"Good Sermon, Brother!"

A Concise Guide to Preaching Good Sermons.

Jeff Mullins

To My Friend Charlie,

Happy reading. I hope
this book is of benefit
to you

Frank E. Huff

7-20-13

Jeff Mullins

ISBN-13:
978-1490423562

ISBN-10:
1490423567

Cover Photo: pictures Jeff Mullins preaching at a church in Mugumu, Tanzania in 2009 along with Joseph Musuma Marwa who is translating. Joseph has been instrumental in the formation of the Independent Bible Fellowship Church of Tanzania (IBFCT). The IBFCT organized in order to faithfully preach God's Word as a result of the teaching and encouragement of Steve VanHorn and the ministry of International Training and Equipping Ministries (ITEM).

DEDICATION

This book is dedicated to all who have a heart to understand God through His Word and are willing to diligently study it to be able to faithfully teach it to others.

This work is dedicated to those men who are faithful to God and willing to step into the pulpit to preach even though they are neither "professional" pastors nor formally educated preachers.

- These are the men who understand that as followers of the Lord Jesus they are to be growing personally in their relationship with Jesus and making disciples of all nations.

- These are the men who understand that the task of making disciples includes first understanding God's truth in the Bible themselves and then communicating it to others.

- These are the men who are dedicated enough, courageous enough and committed enough to devote the time and energy necessary to study God's Word carefully and to preach it faithfully.

- These are the men who faithfully serve God to be pleasing to Him without seeking recognition from people but anticipate the day when they will hear the Lord say, "Well done, good and faithful servant."

This book is especially dedicated to the faithful pastors of the Independent Bible Fellowship Church of Tanzania (IBFCT) who, at great personal cost and sacrifice, have committed to faithfully preaching God's Word.

CONTENTS

ACKNOWLEDGMENTS

In the words of the Apostle Paul
I thank Christ Jesus our Lord, who has strengthened me, because He
considered me faithful, putting me into service, . . . the grace of our
Lord was more than abundant, with the faith and love which are found
in Christ Jesus.
1 Timothy 1:12-14

This work is presented with a depth of gratitude to those who have set
an example of good preaching and have invested in my life through
instruction and encouragement to faithfully preach the Word of God.

I am grateful to those who have granted to me the opportunity to
preach almost every Sunday for over two decades. I am grateful to my
wife, Mary and our seven children who have been, and continue to be
a great encouragement.

To those who have endured and scoured through this work at its
various stages to find mistakes and provide recommendations – thank
you. I cannot adequately pay you but assuming this effort glorifies
God, your reward is in heaven – God knows who you are.

INTRODUCTION

This book is based on the premise that it is impossible to faithfully preach or teach the Bible unless the preaching and teaching is based on accurate interpretation.

Although there is a focus on preaching, the majority of this book will benefit anyone who wants to study the Bible for themselves or who serves in teaching the Bible in any capacity.

The first two chapters consider how to assess sermons as good or bad and discusses the problems what is called "Good Sermon, Bad Text." A clear distinction between application and interpretation is emphasized.

Chapters three and four evaluate faulty methods of interpretation and present a method of approach to the Bible that produces consistently accurate interpretations.

The fifth and sixth chapters provide specific helps in determining accurately the interpretation of any passage.

The balance of the material present deal with a variety of practical issues to build sermons and lessons that are clearly built upon the Biblical text.

The words on these pages are offered to you with prayer and a desire to glorify God, to honor His Word and encourage His people to humbly serve Him.

May you be blessed by God through your efforts in reading this book and may God make you an abundant blessing to those you encounter because you have made the effort to preach a "Good Sermon, Brother!"

Chapter 1
The Big Picture
Introduction to Teaching/Preaching the Bible

"Good sermon today, Pastor!" The scene repeats itself like clockwork.

The pastor stands at the back of the church as the people mingle, file out and offer words of encouragement to the pastor. But what do those words mean? Is saying "good sermon" the church goer's way of saying "goodbye" or does he actually mean something?

At times a pastor knows he has preached poorly. Maybe it was because of inadequate preparation. Maybe is was sensitivity tension in the church. Or perhaps trouble at home torpedoed delivery of the message.

Yet, on the days he knows in his heart that he has preached poorly he still hears accolades like "Pastor, that was the best sermon ever!"

Should the pastor embrace the people's affirmations as a compliment or an insult on such occasions? Of course, it may be that the Holy Spirit made a "good" sermon out of a bad one. Or, it may be that the one listening to the sermon is sincere but just has no clue about what constitutes a good sermon.

So what is a good sermon? How can one tell if a sermon is good or bad? If 30 people listen to the same sermon some may conclude it was good. Others may conclude it was bad. Who is right?

Is assessing a sermon good or bad merely a subjective personal evaluation or are there objective criteria? It is probably safe to say that God considers some sermons good and others bad. What criteria might God use?

1

Consider that a good sermon has two fundamental characteristics:

- The content of the sermon is based on accurate interpretation of the Bible, and

- The sermon is communicated effectively to those who hear.[1]

<u>First, Understand The Bible!</u>

The preacher must understand what God has said in order to be able to accurately portray the message to those who will hear. The process involved in coming to understand the Bible is called interpretation. Proper interpretation results in an accurate and correct understanding of what God has said. Interpretation is concerned with what God said to the people He was speaking to at that time (then) and in the setting (there) He was speaking to them. Interpretation is concerned with was communicated "then and there". **The correct interpretation of any text will answer the singular question, "_What_ did God say to the original audience?"[2]**

Interpretation is focused on determining "authorial intent". Therefore the interpreter **does not** ask, "_What is God saying to me?_" Nor does he ask "_What is God saying to people today?_" These are good, legitimate and necessary questions. However, the time to ask "_What is God saying to me?_" is not during the interpretation process. Those questions focusing on application of the text to modern people will be asked <u>after</u> the correct interpretation is understood. Asking about personal, or present day, application of the text during the process of interpretation process frequently leads to a wrong conclusions about the meaning of the text. Additionally, when the question is asked, "_What is God saying to me?_" the answers will be as varied as the

---

[1] Effective communication includes mental comprehension as well as understanding how to put into practice the biblical truths that are put forth.

[2] Biblical interpretation is not unique in this way. All interpretation seeks to identify what the original author communicated to the original audience.

persons who are asking it because the question itself solicits a subjective/personal answer.

Asking the wrong question in interpretation leads people to misunderstand the interpretation. This wrong approach to interpretation leads people to say, "Well, that is your interpretation and I see it differently!" An interpretation process that leads to such varied, and often contradictory understandings, undermines the value, authority and validity of the Word of God.

In most instances, there is only one correct interpretation of a given text! A relatively small number of "future looking" prophetic texts include both a short term and a long term fulfillment. One such example is found in Isaiah 7:14 regarding the virgin giving birth to a son. The New Testament makes it clear that this spoke of Jesus, but there was also an immediate, and somewhat different, fulfillment during Isaiah's lifetime. However, even in these instances, the correct interpretation of the Old Testament text, is identified by asking the question "_What_ did God say to the original audience?"

Since the intended meaning of original author does not ever change, it is clear that the correct interpretation should not vary depending on who is doing the interpretation. Regardless of whether the interpreter is a man or woman, a carpenter or an executive, a preacher or a truck driver, each should arrive at the same interpretation. If two people come to different conclusions about the interpretation of a text, then one is incorrect. Both may be incorrect.

To correctly and consistently understand what any Bible text says, a method of interpretation must approach the Word of God as authoritative. The interpreter should purposefully seek to allow God's Word to speak for itself. The interpreter's goal is to "read-out" of the Scripture, rather than to "read-into" it. "Reading out" of the

Scriptures[3] is seeking to understand what the author said and the original audience understood. "Reading into" the Scriptures[4] refers to the natural human tendency to read into the words that are written one's own thoughts, opinions, understanding or beliefs.

Use a Consistent Method for Interpretation

Interpreting the Bible is not really very different than interpreting any other type of communication but, for a variety of reasons, Bible interpretation is frequently approached very different from "normal" communication. Unfortunately, many of these approaches result in inaccurate, inconsistent, contradictory and even wildly strange ideas.

The method of interpretation presented in the following pages strives for consistency, accuracy and an unbiased understanding of each text. The meaning is what the author stated in the words and sentences used. The method that will be presented is called the literal-historical-grammatical method of interpretation. Following is a brief description of the main tenants of this method:

1. Literal means the normal meaning of the language used is sought. The meaning is in what is said, not in something hidden or obscure or written between the lines. Literal interpretation means understanding narrative as narrative, poetry as poetry and allegory as allegory, etc. (Literal does not mean "to take everything literally" when the text obviously includes a figure of speech.)

2. Historical. Since the purpose of Bible interpretation is to determine the meaning which God intended for the original audience, it is important to understand the historical and cultural context in which the words were spoken/written. The

---

[3]   Technically called "exegesis"

[4]   Technically called "eisogesis"

meaning of a text is determined within the historical setting when the words were written.

3. <u>Grammatical</u> - God has communicated with human languages which is comprised of words and sentences. The meaning of words, phrases and sentences is found in the grammatical context. When taken out of context the intended meaning can be easily overlooked, distorted and misunderstood. It is aptly stated, "a text taken out of context is a pretext."

At the end of the interpretive process two goals should be accomplished. The interpreter should be able to summarize[5]:

1. <u>WHAT the author said</u> - The meaning of the text should be stated in one concise sentence that includes identifying who the original author and original audience were.[6] This statement can be called the exegetical idea[7] (or main idea) of the text, and

2. <u>WHY the author said it</u> - The purpose that God had in mind for communicating this message to the people of that day should be expressed in one concise sentence. The purpose statement should also be made in terms of the original author and original audience.

<u>A Graphic Representation of Interpretation</u>

Interpretation can be pictured as pouring everything about the text into the wide mouth of a funnel. A large amount of material, facts and

---

[5] Examples and more explanation will follow as this method of interpretation is explored more fully.

[6] Example: Paul (original author) told the believers at Philippi (original audience) . . . to rejoice always. By including the name of original author and audience in the interpretation of the text the interpreter is forced to answer the right question: "What did the original author say to the original audience?"

[7] "Exegetical" is a term that means to "read out of" The opposite of exegesis is "eisegesis" which refers to reading into the text as meaning.

information are funneled down until the main thing is understood and comes out of the small funnel spout. That end product, in the form of a main idea and purpose statement, are valid and accurate when they capture in summary form what God had to say and why. The process of interpreting the Bible is called "hermeneutics".

Interpretation Requires Work

Interpreting the Bible using this method is hard work. However it is very rewarding, honoring to God and essential to correctly interpreting the text. While there are many tools that can be used in the process, there are no shortcuts to accurate interpretation. Paul told Timothy *"Be diligent to present yourself approved to God as a workman who does not need to be ashamed, accurately handling the word of truth."* (2 Timothy 2:15) James likewise warned *"Let not many of you become teachers, my brethren, knowing that as such we will incur a stricter judgment."* (James 3:1)

These admonitions and warnings should not be overlooked nor dismissed. Neither should the effort required, and the accountability incurred, become an excuse for not studying and teaching/preaching God's Word. The point of these warnings is that great care should be exercised to make sure that the Bible is understood accurately and then communicated clearly. The one who is teaching the Bible is claiming "Thus says the Lord." The preacher must ensure he is actually saying what the Lord has said, and not just giving his own opinion.

So the first criteria to preaching a good sermon is that the preacher must ensure that he has something worthwhile to say. When preaching, that which is worthwhile to say is what God has said.

Second – Communicate the Bible Effectively

Having understood the correct meaning of the text, the preacher has something worthwhile to say. The second thing needed to preach a good sermon is to communicate the message to the contemporary audience in a way they can understand and that applies to their lives the truths of God.

Thus, preparing to preach/teach from the Bible is a two stage process – first interpretation; then formulating how the message will be communicated effectively. This second part relates to application of what was understood in interpretation. Interpretation is the basis for sermon/lesson preparation. Yet, preparing the sermon is, of necessity, both separate and distinct from interpretation. This is because interpretation is rooted in the "then and there" of the Biblical text. The phrase "then and there" refers to the fact that the Biblical text and events happened in the past, "then" and at a different location, "there" as contrasted with those who are currently reading it.

Sermon/lesson preparation (after interpretation) focuses upon how to relate the truths identified by careful interpretation to people living in the "here and now". The phrase "here and now" refers to the fact that preaching is occurring at a modern location "here", and at the present time, "now." The distinction between the "then and there" and the "here and now" is essential in order to first accurately interpret the Scriptures and then also to help people understand today how they should respond to what was said.

There are two common mistakes in preaching/teaching that arise from failing to maintain the interpretation stage separate from the sermon/lesson preparation stage.

The first mistake is to skip the hard work of first interpreting the Scripture text. This happens when the preacher/teacher approaches the Bible text asking, "What does this mean to me?" and begins preparing a sermon/lesson. The result of this approach is that that the message is based on the authority of the preacher rather than the authority of God and His Word.

The second common mistake is that the preacher/teacher does a good job of interpretation leading to a correct interpretation of the text but fails to communicate the truths of God in ways that relate to the people in the audience. This results in an academic presentation of Bible truth that leaves people saying, "Well that was an interesting bunch of information, but so what?" Sermons that communicate the product of interpretation may teach many things, but people's lives are often left untouched by the Word of God.

For this reason the second step in preparing a sermon is to take what has been learned in the interpretation process and to make a plan for how to present it in a way that, 1) preserves God's original message and, 2) communicates how it applies to the lives of people who will hear. This second step is sometimes called "homiletics" which means the art of preparing sermons.

A Graphic Representation of Sermon/Lesson Preparation

The second step, sermon preparation, is built upon the first step, interpretation. This second step can also be pictured as a funnel. However, the funnel in the second step is up-side-down with the little end up.

The actual sermon preparation process begins with the main idea and the purpose statement of the biblical text identified as the product of interpretation. Sermon preparation begins by restating the "then and there" product of interpretation in terms of the "here and now" lives that the audience of the sermon can relate to. The result will be that the sermon content and purpose is clearly based upon what God has said and is applicable to the lives of people in the audience.

Considering the whole process, the two funnels combine at the narrowest points and result in an hour glass appearance. The top half of the hour glass is interpretation that results in two concise statements about the meaning of the text. The bottom half of the hour glass starts with a restatement of the product of interpretation and from these expands and fills in material to construct the sermon. In the narrow neck of the hour glass is the transition point from the "then and there" of interpretation to the "here and now" of application of sermon preparation. By following this process there can be a high degree of confidence that the sermon is based on what God has actually said – and that makes for a good sermon.

Before looking at these two stages of sermon preparation in more detail it will be helpful to consider how some pastors preach what is called "good sermon, bad text".

Chapter 2

Good Sermon – Bad Text

"*Hey, you're missing the point!*" When attempting to communicate something important, it can be frustrating to be misunderstood.

Sometimes misunderstanding is the fault of the one speaking. Sometimes it is the fault of the one listening. Sometimes it is the fault of both. Effective communication depends on two people – the one sending the communication and the one receiving the communication. No matter where the blame may lie, if the point is not understood by the recipient then the communication has been ineffective.

In the Bible though, God is the one speaking[8]. When God speaks it must be acknowledged that He has clearly and effectively communicated.

If God is not correctly understood, the fault surely does not lie with God. It is serious when a person fails to understand correctly what God has said. It is even more serious when the person who fails to understand clearly propagates their error by teaching it to others.[9] No one appreciates having their words misunderstood or

---

[8]   It should be noticed that both the human author of scripture and God are considered the author/writer of the Bible. This is because the Bible is inspired, written by human authors who spoke/wrote as they were carried along by the Spirit of God (I Timothy 3:16-17; 2 Peter 1:20-21)

[9]   James 3:1 Let not many of you become teachers, my brethren, knowing that as such we will incur a stricter judgment.

misrepresented. How much more significant is it when God's Word is misunderstood and subsequently misrepresented to others.

There is shame and dishonor before God that comes to the one who is not careful to correctly understand and present God's Word.

> 2 Timothy 2:15 says "Be diligent to present yourself approved to God as a workman who does not need to be ashamed, accurately handling the word of truth."

Interpreting and communicating the Bible is surely a weighty responsibility. The gravity of the task should not cause anyone to neglect studying nor avoid teaching or preaching the Word. Every Christian is tasked with growing spiritually themselves and making disciples of others – both of which requires studying, understanding and communicating God's Word. Instead of causing avoidance of God's Word, the weightiness of handling accurately the Bible should provide a motivation and encourage diligent study to get it right.

Diligence in interpretation begins by asking the right question, which is, "What did God say?" Notice that the question is not "What *is* God saying?" but "What *did* God say?" This distinction is subtle but monumental in its significance. The goal of interpretation is to understand what God said to the original audience in the past, in that historical setting.

The natural human tendency is to approach the Scriptures thinking that we already know what we will find written there. It is common to have in mind a predetermined and specific practical application of the text to be presented to the contemporary audience even before the text is considered. When this occurs, the preacher has decided in advance what he wants to tell people, and turns to the Scriptures to give authority to what he wants to say. This is an upside down and backward approach to Bible interpretation that really is not interpreting the Bible at all.

Of course, personal and practical application is good and necessary. However, making application without careful interpretation first is often what leads many to a wrong understanding of a particular text. Consequently, many people overlook, ignore and neglect the vital distinction between interpretation and application. Proper interpretation is the basis for appropriate application. Putting application too early in the process is like "not getting the point" but marching off presumptuously and doing something anyway.

When sermons, or Bible lessons, are based upon inadequate interpretation of the Bible it results in a bad sermon or a bad lesson. After all, if the sermon or the lesson teaches something from a particular Bible text that God never intended that text to communicate, it is obviously a bad sermon. Indeed, the meaning of the text is determined by the author of the text. Lack of careful and accurate interpretation leading to a "bad sermon" is a shameful thing.

However, many Bible preachers and teachers fall back on their broad, and generally accurate, understanding of theology as a safety net from teaching error. In such cases error may not be taught, but the truth that is taught does not originate from the text itself, but from some other place(s).

In such cases, the message may be considered a "theologically correct sermon" because it was consistent with the theological truth taught in the whole of the Bible. However, the sermon preached is based on a general understanding of the truth of the Bible rather than specifically on the truth taught in the text that is in focus. Of such a sermon it could be said, "good sermon, bad text!"

"Good sermon, bad text" means that the preacher effectively preached, he did not preach error, he kept people's attention and he gave some suggestions on how to put the truth into practice. It could be rightly ask, "How could anyone fault that?" The fault lies in that, although he did not teach false doctrine, he did not teach what **"that text"** taught. In other words, his overall understanding of Scripture kept him from saying that which was untrue, but what he presented was not true of the particular text in view.

> **When a preacher preaches "good sermon, bad text" he misrepresents the Scriptures. Although, on the surface it may seem that no harm is done, the truth is that the preacher has done great harm.**

The harm in the "good sermon, bad text" is that the preacher has unwittingly snatched the Word of God out of the people's hands and he has put it out of their reach. The one listening may think that the sermon was great and that the preacher is awesome. However, the preacher sends the people away with the impression that "only preachers can understand what God's Word says." The preacher is reading good theology into the passage, rather than seeking to let the passage speak what the passage says. This is reading into the text, even though what is being read into the text is something that may be true in and of itself.

In a sense, the preacher points to the text, saying, "this is what God says," when the text he points to is not saying what the preacher says it is saying. God may have said it in another place, but it is not what God said in this place. Consequently, the person listening looks at the text, hears what the preacher says and concludes that there is no way he could ever understand that text to be saying what the preacher says it is saying. Yet, "the preacher is "the preacher", and the preacher is more knowledgeable and educated and what he says, sounds right." The result is that people hearing a "good sermon" from a "bad text" are actually discouraged from studying the Bible themselves because the sermon preached does not match the words of the text.

When the preacher presents good theology from the wrong text it is as if he has elevated himself to the position of a little pope. The preacher becomes the one who has the final say about what Scripture mean, because obviously no one else can understand it. People think "Never, in 1000 years, could I have understood that text to say those things." The truth is that in many cases the text did not say those things. Instead, the preacher/teacher has read them into the text.

Admittedly, a "good sermon, bad text" is better than a bad sermon. It is always better to teach good theology and biblical truth than it is to teach error or just stories, or political correctness, or . . . . Yet, it is much better to preach a good sermon from a good text.

To preach a "good sermon, good text" the preacher must first understand the correct interpretation of the text and then prepare the sermon based on what that text says. There needs to be a clear correlation between what the person hearing the sermon reads in the Bible text and what the preacher is saying from the same Bible text. The preacher points to the text, saying "this is what God says" and the person in the audience looks at the text and concludes "that is what God says" because that is what the text says. When the sermon is based on the correct interpretation of the text those who hear the sermon will be encouraged to study the Scriptures. When it is obvious that the sermon is based on the text the preacher demonstrates how anyone can read, interpret, understand and apply the Scriptures. Good preaching provides an example of careful and accurate interpretation enabling anyone who applies himself diligently following that example, to accurately interpret.

Another great danger in the "good sermon, bad text" methodology is that the correctness of the sermon is only as good as the preacher's theological understanding. If the preacher has erroneous theology, and that theology is read into the text, then the result is a "bad sermon and a bad text". On the other hand, the preacher who preaches from the text itself has an additional safeguard from teaching error. If the truth of the text is what is always preached, then there will never be a sermon that teaches the erroneous theology. The reality is that "good sermon, bad text" is the product of dogmatic interpretation[10]. In such cases the sermon will only be faithful to the truth of God to the extent the teacher/preacher grasps true dogma (teaching).

Preachers and teachers have a grave responsibility to preach and teach the truth of God in a way that is accurate and makes it clear that God is the authority. Without accurate interpretation and messages based clearly upon the text the preacher/teacher becomes an authority that snatches the Bible from the people's hands. When this happens, people become dependent upon the "authority" to tell them what it means.

To put the Bible in the hands of God's people the preacher/teacher must first interpret the Bible and then teach from each text what that text says. In this way the people learn the truth of God and also have demonstrated in each lesson/sermon the correlation between the truth and text.

To correctly interpret the Scriptures a methodology must be used that is consistent with the nature of the Bible itself and that is applied consistently. Unfortunately, there are many faulty approaches to interpretation that have been historically present in the church and pose significant dangers today. Obviously, if the interpretation is wrong, then the sermon/lesson will not be true to the Bible either.

The next chapter will provide an overview of some of the more common faulty methods of interpretation.

---

[10]   The next chapter defines and discusses the errors associated with dogmatic, and other faulty, interpretation methods.

Chapter 3

Faulty Methods of Interpretation
Bad Interpretation = Bad Sermon = Bad Preacher

Correct interpretation relies on the interpreter understanding basic facts about the Bible and utilizing an interpretation method that is consistent with the nature of the Bible.[11] Among the foundational truths about the Bible that are indispensable to accurate interpretation are the following[12]:

- The Bible is God's Word, not just a book.

- The Bible is Revelation from God

- The Bible is Inspired by God

- The Bible is Authoritative

The nature of the Bible requires that the interpreter approach it with an attitude of submission and humility. The authority of the Word of God stands in judgment over people rather than the interpreter's understanding and intellect standing in judgment upon God's Word. The Word of God must be allowed to change what the interpreter believes rather than the interpreter approaching the Bible with an inclination to find there what is already believed.

---

[11] 2 Timothy 2:15 Be diligent to present yourself approved to God as a workman who does not need to be ashamed, accurately handling the word of truth. "Accurately handling" means to cut straight or rightly divide. This should be understood as the task of the interpreter is to work hard to understand what the Bible says.

[12] These terms will be explained in the following pages.

Throughout history, and common today, some people approach the Bible denying its nature which results in the interpreter's authority over shadowing the authority of God and His Word. Awareness of faulty methods will help interpreters honor God by avoiding common pitfalls in interpretation that lead to incorrect understandings.

Below is a summary of five common faulty methods of interpretation. The error of some of these methods is easy to see and avoid. Others pose clear dangers but are more subtle because human pride makes everyone susceptible to them, even those who are committed to careful submission to God in interpretation.

ALLEGORICAL - this faulty method of interpretation has as a basic premise that all Scripture is to be read and interpreted as if it were an allegory.

> The problem with this method is that interpreting something the author did not write as allegory, as if it were allegory, makes the text say whatever the interpreter wants rather than what the author intended. The interpreter, not the Bible, becomes the authority with this method.

An allegory is an extended comparison that does not use words such as "like" or "as." In allegories one symbol represents one other thing. Allegories are stories in which each person, object or incident is intended to convey some symbolic significance. The meaning of an allegory is to be found in the symbolism, not in the actual words.

- The Bible does contain allegories. When it is clear that the author wrote an allegory, the text should be interpreted as allegory (One example of the use of allegory as a literary type in the Bible is what is called the parable of the "sower" Mt 13:1-23. In the parable each item represents something else –

soils represents men's hearts, seed represent the Word of God, weeds represent the cares of the world, etc).

- If the author did not intend a text as allegory, it should not be interpreted as if it were allegory

- "Allegorizing" is a method of interpretation that interprets a text as if it were an allegory even though it was not intended to be an allegory.

- Allegorical interpretation has been around for a long time.

  ○ A scholar and philosopher named Philo (20-50 B.C.) used allegorical interpretation of the Old Testament.

  ○ In the church age Origen (255 AD), an early church father, allegorized Scripture.

  ○ Augustine (400 AD) used the allegorical method of interpretation. He was the first one to set down rules for interpretation. His views dominated the church during the middle ages.

Although "Allegorizing" is not widely used today as a primary method of interpretation, it is common for individuals and preachers to interpret a text saying that one thing represents another when the author did not intend it that way. This is allegorizing. Allegorizing makes the Scriptures say something that God did not intend.

There are some significant problems with allegorizing Scripture (or any other communication for that matter). The primary problems with allegorizing include:

1. The interpreter can make any text say anything the interpreter can imagine.

2. The text can have unlimited meanings beyond what the author intended.

3. The interpreter's ideas dominate the meaning rather than what God intended.

4. The interpreter, not God or His Word, is the authority.

The only time a text should be interpreted as allegory, is when it is clearly intended by the author to be an allegory. Treating Scripture texts as allegory when they are not allegory leads to erroneous interpretations.

DOGMATIC - the word dogmatic is derived from the Latin word "dogma" which simply means a teaching or a doctrine.

> The problem with the dogmatic method of interpretation is that the interpreter's beliefs determine the interpretation rather than what the author intended.

The basic premise in the dogmatic method of interpretation is that all Scripture is interpreted in harmony with existing and accepted doctrine. Dogmatic interpretation is very common today by individuals, groups and institutions.

Dogmatic interpretation has been historically practiced by the Roman Catholic Church.

(a) A man named Hugo said "first learn what you should believe and then go to Scripture and find it there." (In this case he meant to learn from the church and her traditions what you believe)

(b) At the Council of Trent (1545-1563) the Roman Church became firmly entrenched in the dogmatic approach as a reaction to the protestant reformation. They embraced what is called "The analogy of faith" which states that the Bible is interpreted in accordance with the true faith. (i.e. church doctrine).

Many churches and individuals practice this method.

   (a) It is an approach that is both subtle and deceptive.

   (b) The dogmatic approach is behind a practice called "proof texting."

      i. Proof texting looks for texts that support a particular doctrine rather than approaching the text to learn what it says and allowing it to speak for itself.

      ii. Proof texting often disregards the context of a sentence or verse or phrase to force the text to say what is desired rather than what the author intended.

2. After the protestant reformation there was a period of confessions and creeds which tended toward dogmatic interpretation.

The problem associated with the dogmatic method of interpretation is that accepted doctrine is considered more authoritative than the inspired Scriptures.

Although doctrinal statements may be helpful, the Scriptures have the ultimate authority; Church doctrine and doctrinal statements should be subjected to the Bible, not the other way around.

NATURALISTIC - The basic premise of this faulty method is that Scripture must be interpreted in a way consistent with modern reason and that can be accepted by the rationalistic, scientific mind.

    The problem with the naturalistic method of interpretation is that human reason is more authoritative than God and God's Word.

This method demands alternative explanations for anything that is considered unreasonable or unscientific by the interpreter. Consequently miracles and predictive prophecy recorded in the Bible need alternative explanations. This method is also called "Anti-Supernaturalism." Naturalism's basis is that God does not do miracles and that the right explanation is determined by science.

1. This method arose after the middle ages during what was called the "Reawakening" following a period when super-naturalism and superstition prevailed. Following the middle ages people became "rationalist and humanistic" in their thinking.

2. The 1700s were called the "Age of Reason" when rational thinking prevailed and man became central (Humanism).

3. The Scriptures came to be interpreted in a way that is "most reasonable to the rationalistic and humanistic mind" excluding the miraculous and divine.

4. During this time Albert Switzer wrote - "The Quest for the Historical Jesus" – According to Switzer, Jesus did not do miracles.

The naturalist method of interpretation has obvious problems, including that:

1. It is founded on the premise of unbelief and that the miracles recorded in the Bible simply are not true.

2. It denies that God, the Creator, is greater than the creature and creation.

3. It denies Jesus, the greatest miracle of all (ie.virgin birth, prophetic prophesies, resurrection)

4. It elevates the reason of man over the authority of God and His Word.

5. It diminishes interpretation to nothing more than identifying errors in the Bible.

The naturalistic approach to interpretation is a position of human pride rather than humility and submission before God. It is impossible to strain out Jesus' miracles w/o straining out Christ who is the greatest miracle of all. Accurate interpretation of the Bible begins with recognizing the supremacy of God and the accuracy and authority of God's Word. The naturalistic approach to interpretation denies both.

SUBJECTIVE - the basic premise of this faulty method of interpretation is that the meaning of Scripture is found not in the words of Scripture but in the inner revelation which one receives when reading and interacting with the Scriptures.

> The fundamental problem with the subjective method is that the meaning of Scripture is determined by the experience of the one reading and has no relationship with the author's intent.

This method essentially ignores any historical meaning the author intended. The subjective method simply asks, "What does it mean to me personally, today?"

1. Subjective interpretation puts emphasis on the personal inner light

   (a) In the wake of the protestant reformation tendencies toward dogmatic interpretation had resulted in an impersonal and a "dead orthodoxy" for many.

(b) People's desire for a real relationship with God gave rise to a movement which was anti-creedal, anti-theology and experience oriented.

(c) Revelation from God to individuals, with or without the Scriptures, became the emphasis.

2. The personal inner light became the authority rather than Scripture within this movement. (Today when people say, "Well, this is what it means to me." and considers that authoritative, it is an example of subjective interpretation.)

3. The words of the Bible no longer are considered <u>to be</u> the Word of God but rather they <u>become</u> the Word of God when a person is enlightened by them.

The subjective method views Scripture as one means of having a personal experience with God. Personal experience, whether arising from the Bible or other means, is considered the authority rather than the Bible. Since technically, the goal of this method is only the "personal application" (what God says to me), in essence any real interpretation of the Bible is skipped altogether. The application is dependent totally upon the person doing the supposed interpretation. There is no limit to the number of meanings. Every meaning is considered equally valid, even when it is in total conflict with another person's meaning or the clear statements of the Bible.

Contrary to the tenants of this method, God has communicated propositional truth with meaning present in the words of the Scriptures that He intends people to understand, believe and obey. Without a correct interpretation it is impossible to come to correct application.

Additionally, the natural inclination of man's heart is self centered and self serving. Consequently, a personal subjective interpretation usually leads away from the truth rather than into the truth.

MYTHOLOGICAL - the basic premise of this faulty method is that the New Testament contains only what the early church "thought" about the Christ figure, not the truth about the historical man, Jesus.

> The problem with the mythological approach is that it denies the Father and the Son and is a position of pure unbelief.

The mythological method asserted that the gospels contain mostly "myths" rather than actual history of Jesus. This is related to the naturalistic method and considers that anything that is contrary to a modern scientific world view is merely mythology. This method considers the role of the interpreter is to be a literary sleuth to demythologize the Bible – that is, to separate the true facts from the "myths" so that it can be expressed to the modern rational mind.

1. When this approach is used, 9/10ths of the Bible is lost in the surgery.

2. It is based on a position of unbelief and assumes that the Bible is full of errors.

3. Man becomes the authority to pick and choose what is genuine and what is fabricated.

The mythological approach to interpretation is man standing in judgment on the Bible in a literary form criticism rather than an honest attempt to understand what it says and means.

Summary of Faulty Methods of Interpretation

Serious students of the Bible will easily reject some of these faulty approaches to the Bible recognizing that they clearly arise from unbelief. However, lack of a clear and consistent method of interpretation that embraces the authority of God in His Word leaves many Bible students very susceptible to the dogmatic or subjective interpretation approaches at times. Doctrine is important, but the emphasis on a particular teaching can easily become dogmatic rather than Biblical in its foundation. Likewise, the tendency toward subjective interpretation is an ever present danger. Interpretation must rest on what the particular text says, not on what is already believed nor what the interpreter thinks or feels.

Chapter 4

A Reliable Interpretation Method
Understanding What God Has Said

The nature of interpretation is that it begins with what will be interpreted! Interpretation begins with what was said, what was spoken, what was written. Interpretation does not begin with a topic, theme, idea, conclusion, or point to be made. Interpretation seeks to understand the inherent meaning that the author, writer or speaker intended to communicate. Interpretation depends on grasping the intent of the one expressing the communication. Interpretation is a journey of discovery.

Contrary to the very nature of interpretation, many Bible students begin with a message they want to give, an idea they want to communicate or a point they want to make. If the "outcome" is predetermined in the mind of the one supposedly doing the "interpretation", it should not be surprising that "reading into the text" is a common occurrence.

A Valid Starting Point For Interpretation

Before interpretation begins a text must be selected that will be the basis of the sermon. The preacher begins, not with a subject, not with an idea, not with a sermon, but with a Biblical text. Admittedly the text may be selected because of an idea or subject in mind based on the preachers prior understanding of the text. However, great self discipline is required to allow the text to speak for itself and to avoid reading back into the text preconceived ideas.[13]

So, sermon/lesson preparation begins with the selection of a text in the Bible. Until proficient in the process, it is probably best to select a text containing at least 2-3 verses but not more than a chapter. This size of texts usually contains enough material from which a sermon can be prepared, but not so much material that identification of the main idea of the texts is obscured by an overwhelming amount of information to sift through.

After the interpreter becomes skilled and practiced in interpretation and sermon/lesson preparation it is feasible to study whole books or sections of the Bible and to prepare and present sermons/lessons on them. However, for the beginner, and the unpracticed, it is best to bite off a smaller portion.

Overview of Interpretation

After the text has been chosen, the interpretation process begins. Interpretation seeks to understand the text by a process which will include in part:

- Reading the text repeatedly (memorizing the text if it is a short passage)

- Making and recording observations about the text

- Meditating upon the text[14]

---

[13]   This book focuses on preparing sermons/lessons that would be considered "expository." This means that the sermon preached is primarily from a single text and that the sermon explains that text and applies that text to the hearers. Other sermon forms may be legitimate but it is suggested that the expository sermon should comprise the bulk of sermons anyone preaches.

[14]   Meditation refers to purposefully focusing mental attention on the text as a whole and the details of the text. Contrary to meditation of eastern mystic religions, meditation is filling one's mind with what God says, not emptying it and allowing it to be filled with whatever may come. Biblical meditation may include reading and re-reading, memorizing the text

- Recording thoughts, ideas and questions

- Recording possible illustrations and applications.

- Outlining the text (perhaps based on a grammatical diagram)

- Summarizing the text in two concise statements (of meaning and purpose)

Interpreting the Bible is kind of like a cow eating and digesting grass. First graze. Then rest. Then regurgitate. Chew on it some more. Rest a while. Regurgitate – chew . . . swallow, repeat . . . repeat. Repeat! The picture is clear. There is no substitute for spending significant time, and repeated periods of time, studying the text. Time and thought are indispensable if the Bible is going to be understood correctly.

Although everyone may not be a preacher, every Christian should be a student of God's Word. Every Christian is to make disciples which includes "teaching them to observe" all that Jesus commanded.[15] The process summarized above, and detailed in the material that follows, will prove very helpful for all who strive to correctly understand and communicate God's Word clearly.

A blessed byproduct of spending the time needed to correctly interpret God's Word is that the interpreter, through study, exposes himself to God and God's Word. God first uses His Word to do a work in the life of the individual who studies and then God uses that individual to

---

or portions of it, asking one's self how the text applies to this situation or that situation or this role or that role, etc. Meditation includes what is often referred to as observing the text and questioning the text. Questions would include the who, what, where, when, how questions. Observing the text includes placing it before you and "picking at it" to understand it intimately.

[15] Matthew 28:19 "Go therefore and make disciples of all the nations, baptizing them in the name of the Father and the Son and the Holy Spirit, 20 teaching them to observe all that I commanded you; and lo, I am with you always, even to the end of the age."

bring His Word to the life of another individual so He can do His work there too.

Interpretation with Humility

Any valid method of interpretation must humbly submit to God and His Word. It must approach Scripture as a Revelation[16] from God, Inspired by God and Authoritative in one's life. The method must bring the interpreter's every thought, every belief, and every experience into question and subjection, allowing God's Word to have the final say. Such a submissive approach to interpretation is not intellectual suicide. Rather, it simply recognizes that God's Word is the authority, and as it says in Romans 3:4 ". . . let God be found true, though every man be found a liar. . .," Without faith in the accuracy and truthfulness of the Bible, any approach to interpretation is doomed to failure. Faith is a prerequisite to interpreting correctly and understanding the truth of God's Word.[17]

The method presented here is one which sincerely, honestly and humbly seeks to learn what God has said for the purposes of knowing the truth, believing the truth and obeying the truth. Rather than having a particular name, this method of interpretation is identified by its various elements as the Literal-Historical-Grammatical Method of interpretation. As the method is explained, it should become evident that this method is not unique to the Bible and is universally used to interpret both ancient and modern communications. Although more detail will follow, this chapter introduces and gives a summary overview of this method of interpretation.

---

[16] The word "revelation", and other terms, are defined below

[17] 1 Corinthians 2:14 But a natural man does not accept the things of the Spirit of God, for they are foolishness to him; and he cannot understand them, because they are spiritually appraised.

The Focus of Interpretation

The correct interpretation of any text (biblical or otherwise) answers two simple questions:

- "What did the original author intend the original hearer or reader to understand?"

- and, "Why did the author say it?"

As mentioned previously, one of the biggest temptations is to ask, and then attempt to answer, the wrong questions during the interpretation process. Asking, "What does it means to me?" is an interpretive mistake leading to Subjective Interpretation – that is, seeking a personal-subjective application rather than an objective interpretation. Application is very important. However, application, when it is not based on a valid interpretation, results in each man being the authority rather than God. Subjective interpretation ultimately leads to varied and diverse interpretations resulting in "every man doing what is right in his own eyes." The Bible book of Judges makes it clear that this is not pleasing to God.

- The work of the interpreter is to: **understand** and **explain** the **intended thought** of the author
  - as disclosed in the **language** used, and
  - as understood in its **normal literary meaning,** and
  - within the **historical context** as it was written.

(know what was said and why it was said)

Interpretation Based on Nature of Bible

The belief that the Bible is God's Word has significant implications for how it should be interpreted. Before looking specifically at the components of this suggested method, it will be beneficial to consider some of the implications of the Bible being God's Word will have on interpretation. Since the Bible is God's Word it can be expected that there will be:

- Biblical Unity - The entire Bible, while having great diversity, is all one book with a unified source and message. The implications of Biblical unity include:
  - The Bible is free from error and does not contradict itself.
  - Each text will be in harmony with the whole Scripture.
  - All Scripture is used to understand any Scripture. (Analogy of Scripture)

- Biblical Authority - The Bible must be interpreted consistently with its nature as the inspired, revealed and authoritative Word of God.

- Biblical Inspiration - the Holy Spirit guided the human writers of Scripture even to their choice of words, so that what they wrote truly expressed the mind of God and can be accepted as the very words of God. 2 Timothy 3:16 and 2 Peter 1:20-21.
  - Because the Bible was written in a known human language, common to the writer and the intended recipients, it is possible to accurately determine the intended meaning of the author and what the original audience understood.

- Biblical Revelation - the act of God by which He disclosed to men truth which man had not previously known by unaided reason or observation. Ex. 20:1, I Corinthians 2:6-16

- Biblical Authority - the Bible is God's Word and, therefore, the final authority for the Christian in all matters of religious belief and practice. Implications include:
  - It is impossible to treat the Bible casually just like any other book.
  - Interpreting must be with humility and in dependence on the Holy Spirit.

- ○ The Bible judges people, cultures and reason; people cannot stand in judgment on the Bible.
- ○ The Bible is to be applied and obeyed, not just studied academically.
- ○ The language (words, sentences and grammar) of the Bible merits great respect and care.

The elements of the method of interpretation presented here are based upon, and consistent with, the nature of the Bible.

Elements of Biblical Interpretation

The Literal-Historical-Grammatical Method of interpretation includes basic principles and components consistent with the nature of the Bible as God's Word.

LITERAL - The Bible should be interpreted literally (normally as any written language).

The literal principle is based on the understanding that God has communicated in a way that people can understand. When God spoke, His intent was that people would understand what He was saying and that they would respond accordingly.

> It is preferable to use the word "normal" rather than "literal" to describe this component of interpretation. The idea is that the interpreter must look for the normal meaning of Scripture rather than some mystical or hidden meaning.

The normal/literal principle of interpretation is commonly used in understanding communication of every kind.

- Newspapers are read and understood as a newspaper.
- Comic strips are read and understood as comic strips.
- Dictionaries are read and understood as dictionaries.

- Owner's manuals are read and understood as technical manuals.
- Novels are read and understood as novels
- Poetry is read and understood as poetry
- Satire as satire (the list could go on and on)

Obviously, to read satire as if it were a technical manual, or to read a novel as if it were a newspaper would render a meanings far different from what was intended by the author. So it is with the Bible.

The Bible contains different types of literature. Each type must be understood in its normal ways, consistent with the intent of the author.

To interpret Scriptures "literally" means that the type of literature is identified and understood consistent with it's type – normally:

- Narrative is to be understood as narrative.
- Poetry in the Bible is to be understood as poetry.
- Figures of speech as figures of speech.,
- etc.

    The Bible has teaching passages with direct commands. There are passages in which there is sarcasm. Passages that are literal should be interpreted literally - they say exactly what they mean and mean exactly what they say. However, some passages are figurative and the meaning is in the picture drawn by the words, not the words themselves. Examples include the parables of Jesus. They are often easy to identify as parables because the Bible specifically says they are parables. Thus it is appropriate to interpret them as parables.

    Following the literal principle of interpretation helps one to understand the correct meaning of ancient literature, including the Bible, as well as modern communications. Failing to observe the literal principle of interpretation leads to errors in understanding the intended, which is the correct, meaning.

Generally speaking, the literal principle suggests that the Scriptures "say what they mean and mean exactly what they say." Even when there are figures of speech and allegory and sarcasm – the meaning is found in the intended meaning of the author as he would be normally (according to the literary style or genre) understood.

The importance of this principle should be obvious. Imagine ten people who think the meaning of a text is found hidden behind the words trying to interpret the same text of Scripture.

- What are the chances that any two people would identify the same hidden meaning?

- Which of the different, perhaps contradictory interpretations is right?

- What is the authority for saying one interpretation is right and another wrong?

   ****The literal principle is based on the understanding that God has communicated in a way that people can understand. When God spoke, His intent was that people would understand what He was saying and that they would respond accordingly. *****

HISTORICAL - The Bible should be interpreted in a way which takes into account the historical setting and context that surrounded the original message.

   Words are not spoken in a vacuum. The meaning of a statement is understood as it relates to the surrounding events, circumstances and situations when it was made. In almost all cases, the historical setting for a particular biblical text has been provided in the context, or in another related passage of Scripture. For example, the book of Acts provides the historical background for Paul's relationship to the Galatian churches and provides insight into the letter he wrote to them (Galatians).

The significance of the historical setting to the intended meaning of a statement/text can be easily illustrated. Consider, for example, how the exact same statement can mean very different things depending on the historical setting in which the same statement was made. For example:

A man says to his wife, "Oh! I really love you."

Situation #1 – the man and woman are arguing and angry and cannot agree. In the heat of the argument when the wife says that he is supposed to love her, the man shouts sarcastically, "Oh! I REALLY love you!"

Situation #2 – after a scrumptious dinner and a romantic evening, the man, just before falling off to sleep whispers into his wife's ear, "Oh! I really love you."

The words are exactly the same but the meanings are polar opposite. The historical context is crucial to correctly understanding what has been said. The reason why something was said within the historical context, dramatically impacts the interpretation.

GRAMMATICAL - The bible should be interpreted in a normal fashion, taking into account the meaning of the words as used in sentences, in the language used by the author, as understood by the intended audience.

When God communicated, He chose to do so using the language of the people to whom He was communicating (with rare exception). God used the sounds, letters and words that were understood by the people to whom He was speaking so that they could comprehend what was said.

Interpretation is understanding the meaning of the combination of words that God used, as intended by the speaker/author and as understood by the original audience. The meaning is in the words and their relationship to one another. Thus, interpretation is understanding the ordinary meaning of language as contained in the words and sentences.

When God communicated through the agency of the human author, He used the precise words that He wanted in the precise way that He wanted. Successful communication occurred when the recipients understood what God intended. The transfer of that information was by means of words.

In some ways it seems extremely simplistic to say that the task of the interpreter is to understand the meaning and relationship of the words with which God spoke to the original audience. God did not intend to convey several different meanings, but rather one. That one meaning is what the interpreter needs to identify.

The meanings of words are determined by the grammatical context of how they are used in a sentence in their relationship to one another.

For example, what does the word "board" mean? The word "board" can have one of many diverse meanings depending on how it is used in the context of the sentence.

"On my way to a <u>board</u> meeting I ran over a <u>board</u> and the nail in it punctured my tire. So got on <u>board</u> a bus and paid the fare spending the money I intended to use for my room and <u>board</u>."

In this example the same word "board" is used four times and each time it has a different meaning determined by the grammatical context of the word in relationship to the other words in the sentence.

The context of a word determines its meaning and the combined meaning of words depend on their grammatical relationship in sentences.

So it is with the Bible. Each word has a grammatical context within the sentence in which it is found. The context of sentences is the paragraph and the paragraph has a context within the Biblical book.

Although the Bible is divided into chapter and verse divisions, these should be ignored for the sake of interpretation since the context and flow of thought often overlap verse and chapter divisions.

There is another principle of interpretation based on the nature of the Bible. It is called the principle of Progressive Revelation. This principle arises from the fact that God did not disclose all the truth in the Bible at one time. Rather, He began by revealing some truth, adding gradually to it over many centuries until the revelation of truth was completed. When interpreting Scripture it is important to understand and consider that later revelation built upon previous revelation. However, recipients of earlier revelation did not have the content of the revelation that would be given later. For example, Paul knew more than David and David knew more than Moses.

Interpretation of something Moses said should not read into the text something that Paul said many centuries later. The principle of progressive revelation is just one additional precaution to ensure the interpretation seeks the author's intent and is not reading into the text something revealed later, even though it is true.

Chapter 5

Grammatical Diagrams and Sentence Outlines

Caution: This chapter may be a bit technical for some. Please feel free to skip over this chapter altogether if it becomes in any way discouraging or overwhelming. You can always come back to it later if you like. However, for those who are ready to dig deeper into the Word of God and work harder to carefully understand, this chapter may prove very profitable.

Interpreting the Bible is admittedly a mammoth task with a great responsibility. The job seems so huge that it is sometimes hard to know where to begin. The size of the task can be so overwhelming for some that they never get started.

Bible Interpretation is kind of like eating an elephant. "How do you eat an elephant?" The answer, "One bite at a time." Just like you eat anything else. Each text is like eating an elephant one bite at a time. In the end, each piece of the Scripture text has been considered and the interpreter understands how all the pieces fit together.

At the end of the interpretation process the Bible text can be summarized in two succinct summary statements, 1) the exegetical (main) idea and 2) purpose of the text. These summarizing statements are developed based on analysis and understanding of the parts of the text and grasping how they fit together and relate to one another. Some parts of each text are major parts, others parts are minor. Some the parts are primary and other secondary.

Some parts are structurally substantial and others are fine finishing touches.

The exegetical statement summarizes what the text says in terms of the original author and audience. The exegetical purpose states why the author said what he said. These two statements were represented earlier as what comes out of the small funnel spout at the end of the interpretation process. Arriving at these two summary statements require the interpreter to study, analyze, separate and consider all the elements of the text until it is fully understood. A fully understood text can be summarized in a single statement – the exegetical idea (or the main idea of the text).

Among the many tools and methods available to the interpreter, two stand out as especially helpful in separating the main parts of the texts from the secondary parts of the text. These two related tools are grammatical diagramming and text outlining. Outlining and diagramming are methods which are helpful in gaining an understanding about the relationship between different parts of a particular Bible text. Both the outline and diagram serve to arrange the text graphically so the "big bones" in the text become clear and to show how the secondary parts relate to them.

Grammatical diagramming identifies the various parts of the sentences in the text and graphically arranges them so that it is clear what the main thought of each sentence is. It also arranges the modifiers and secondary parts of the sentences to show how they relate to the main thought and to one another. Grammatical diagramming requires at least a minimal understanding of the basic parts of speech used in sentences.[18]

---

[18] Appendix F in this book offers a basic description of the various parts of grammar for those who need assistance the the parts of speech and how they relate to each other.

Diagramming provides the Bible interpreter another significant benefit since it demands a significant amount of focused time and attention be given to the text details and the relationship of its parts. For some interpreters, this forced discipline of concentration on the text is the greatest benefit and aid toward understanding the text. In other words, diagramming forces the interpreter to "chew the cud".

While diagramming focuses on the grammatical relationship of the parts of the text, outlining focuses more on the flow of thought in the text than the actual grammar. Obviously though, they are related since the grammar dictates the thoughts.

Outlining the text is arranging the text into a graphic display of thought to thought relationship of the different parts of the text. An outline of the text may be completed either after completing a diagram or independent from diagramming.

Following is an example of a textual outline and grammatical diagram based on Galatians 5:16-18.

> But I say, walk by the Spirit, and you will not carry out the desire of the flesh. For the flesh sets its desire against the Spirit, and the Spirit against the flesh; for these are in opposition to one another, so that you may not do the things that you please. But if you are led by the Spirit, you are not under the Law.

An outline of the text may look something like this:

1. Walk by the Spirit
   (a) You will not carry out the desires of the flesh
2. The flesh is in opposition to the Spirit
   (a) The Spirit is against the flesh
   (b) You may not do the things you please
3. Those led by the Spirit are not under the Law

This is an example of one way the text could be outlined, understanding that there can be slight legitimate variations. In this example there are three main thoughts in the text represented by the three points in the outline 1, 2 & 3.

It is understandable that the choice of Bible translation/version will change the outcome of both outlining and diagramming. For results that are most consistent with the original texts it is highly recommended that a "word for word"[19] translation/version be used. Word for word translations are especially important for grammatical diagramming because those translations attempt to accurately represent the grammar of the original text. Word for word translations attempt to retain as many of the grammatical aspects of the original languages as possible which aids in diagramming accuracy.[20]

Outlining identifies the main thoughts in the text. The main thoughts become the main points in the outline. Secondary, supporting, explaining and modifying thoughts in the text become the sub-points in the outlining. Sub points are placed under the corresponding main points and indented. Sub-sub points can be used as needed to most accurately represent the thought structure of the text.

When using an outline as an interpretive tool, the structure of the text should determine the structure of the outline, not conventionally accepted rules of outlining. The outline lays out and displays the text rather than the text being forced into an artificial outline, form or shape. For example, outlining rules specify that an outline should never have a single sub-point under a main point. Yet for interpretive purposes, this rule can be ignored. Interpretive outlines are to facilitate

---

[19] "Word for word translations would include New American Standard, King James Version and New King James Version.

[20] No matter which translation will be used in preaching, using a word for word translation in the interpretation process will be most helpful to arriving at an accurate understanding of the text.

understanding by the interpreter and artificially forcing the text to fit technical rules of outlining hinder, rather than help, accurate understanding.

Grammatical diagramming looks more carefully at the details of the grammar to identify the sentences, analyze their structure and graphically arrange the parts of speech to show their relationship to one another. Similar to outlining, diagramming positions the main parts of the speech, including the main nouns and verbs, farthest to the left. Secondary thoughts are farther to the right. Modifiers are placed under the parts that are modified using a series of lines and arrows to show the relationships. Parallel parts of speech will align under one another. As with outlining, it is not as important that a certain method or convention for diagramming is followed. What is important though is that it graphically displays the relationship of the words in the sentence to one another.

Unlike outlining, the diagram will include all the words in the text. For this reason diagramming works best on shorter texts, especially for teaching passages in the New Testament epistles. Diagramming offers much less value for narrative passages and many Old Testament texts. Outlining might be a better option for understanding those types of passages.

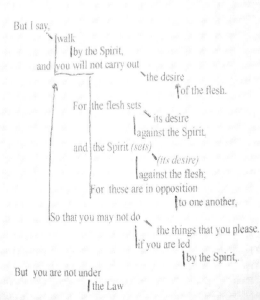

A grammatical diagram of the same text as outlined above (Galatians 5:16-18) would look like this:

Note in the diagram:

- The main nouns/verbs are to the left.

  - "I say" and "you are"

- Parallel thoughts are parallel.

  - Ex: flesh sets, spirit *sets, these are*

- Modifying words and phrases are directly linked to what they modify. ("of the flesh" modifies "desire")

- Word order is ignored in the sentence – the part of speech determines placement

- implied words are added in *italics* (Spirit *sets its desire*)

Significantly, by using the diagram, an outline can be created which is based on the grammar. In an outline based on the grammatical diagram the main points of the outline are derived from the main points in the text as indicated by the grammar. Minor points in the outline can, if desired, reflect the modifiers in the text.

So an outline based on the diagram would look something like this.

1. Paul tells the Galatian believers to walk by the Spirit.
   (a) And they will not carry out the desires of the flesh
   (b) The flesh sets its desire against the Spirit
   (c) The Spirit sets its desire against the flesh
   (d) The flesh and the Spirit are in opposition to one another
      i. So they cannot do the things that please the flesh
2. Paul tells the Galatian believers that they are not under the law
   (a) If they are led by the Spirit

Someone might rightly object that this second outline based on the diagram could have been made without even doing the diagramming. That may be true in this case, but it is not always the case. However, the discipline of diagramming ensures a consistent approach and a detailed look at the text. It is easy to become complacent, lazy and prone to take shortcuts, even with God's Word. Diagramming forces a consistent and honest approach to the text. There is significant benefit to first diagramming the text and then outlining it based on the diagram.

Another advantage of the diagram is the ability gained to see how all the pieces fit together. This level of detail forces the interpreter to think about the relationship of all the words and phrases have to one another. Outlining does not necessarily force one to look at the text in as much detail as diagramming does.

Upon completion of the grammatical diagram the interpreter has identified the main parts (large bones) of the text. By diagramming and/or outlining the text the interpreter gains understanding of the construction of the text to help identify the correct interpretation that can be expressed in the main idea of the text.

Usually it is a small step from a good diagram or outline to identify the main (exegetical) idea of the text.

Chapter 6

The Products Of Interpretations

Upon the completion of the interpretation process the interpreter should be able to concisely summarize the text in two brief sentences stated in terms of the original author and the original audience. These two summary sentences are:

- Exegetical Idea – A sentence summarizing the main idea of the author in the text, and

- Exegetical Purpose – A statement of the purpose the author had for saying what he did.

Identifying the Main Idea of the Text (Exegetical Idea)

The majority of the effort of interpretation is focused on identifying the text's main idea (exegetical idea). No matter if the text is two verses, a chapter, or an entire book of the Bible, the process and the outcome is the same. The interpretation is culminated when a statement of meaning can be made that accurately represents the text.

An analogy of this process may be helpful. Picture the text as a complex hunk of meat, with fat, bones, gristle and lean meat. Throw the hunk into the pot over heat and boil for a long time. The fat melts and floats to the surface, the meat falls off the bones and the bones fall to the bottom of the pot. When the pot is dumped out there will be the soft tissues and the bones. Among the bones there will be the little bones and the big bones. The big bone(s) are the main thing.

The interpretation of a Bible text is like identifying what are the main bones and what are the little bones. Put the verses in a pot and boil it away until the separate parts of the text are clear and the main essence of what the text says stands out from the rest. The big bone(s) comprise the main idea in the text. The main idea, or main point, is not necessarily a section or a sentence taken from the text. Rather, it is a summary statement about the entire text. After thorough study of the text, the interpreter should be able to state in a single concise sentence what God said. The sentence will not include everything that is said in the text, otherwise it would be simply rewriting the text. Instead, it will be a statement in the interpreters words which capture the main thought of the text.

Referring back to the diagram and outline of the Galatians 5 text used in the previous section, it can be seen that the diagram identifies the major pieces that comprise the main point of the text. The main point of the text is closely linked to the main aspects of the diagram. A suggested exegetical idea based on the grammatical diagram and its resultant outline might be:

> Exegetical (Main) Idea: *Paul commands the Galatian believers to walk in the Spirit because they are not under the law.*

Notice that the main idea is in terms of the then and there and identifies both the original author and original audience (Paul – Galatians). The discipline of identifying the original author and audience serves as a check to ensure that it is a statement of interpretation rather than application.

Below are examples of the main ideas from the paragraphs of the book of Jude. It will be most helpful to first read each paragraph and then consider how the exegetical idea captures/summarizes the text.

- Jude 1:1-4 Jude wrote to encourage the believers to contend for the faith.
- Jude 1:5-8 Jude told the believers that the condemnation of the false teachers is sure because it has been pronounced, demonstrated and meted out for the same offenses.
- Jude 1:8-16 Jude explained to the believers that the false teachers care only about themselves and are oblivious to their sure condemnation.
- Jude 1:17-23 Jude told the believers to give care to their own relationship with the Lord and to help others with an attitude of mercy toward them.
- Jude 1:24-25 Jude told the believers that God is the one who is glorified, in everything He accomplishes in their lives.

Observe some significant aspects of each statement of each exegetical idea. Each . . .

- identifies the original audience and the original author (Jude . . . believers).
- is stated in terms of the then and there (not the here and now).
- uses the names and pronouns in the third person, not the first or second. (there are no references to "Me", "I", We or "You")
- concisely summarizes the main thought contained in the text (not every modifying or explanatory aspects of the text is included)

If done well, the exegetical idea for each text sumarizes the main thought that God was communicating through Jude to the people to whom he was writing. By purposefully including the name of the human author and the intended audience in the exegetical idea it encourages the formulation of a statement of interpretation rather than inadvertently slipping into a statement of application.

To determine the main idea of the text the interpreter utilizes a number of analytical and discovery techniques. These include: developing a grammatical diagram of the sentences in the text, outlining the text, performing word studies, comparing cross references, comparing parallel passages, comparing apparent conflicting passages, studying the context, etc. These are all important and each one serves to help come to an accurate understanding of the meaning of the text.

However, of all the methods and tools available the most important, and valuable, is the time spent concentrating on the text. The more time looking at the text, the more time thinking about the text, the more time considering the details of the text, the more thought given to the context of the text . . . the more time and effort spent, the greater the likelihood of accurately interpreting the passage. There is no substitute for focused time![21]

The first product of interpretation will be a statement of the main idea (exegetical idea) in terms of the what the original author said to the original audience. The second product of interpretation is answering the question of "why?" That is, "Why did the author say what he said?"

Identifying the Purpose of the Text - (Exegetical Purpose)

An accurate understanding of what has been said often depends on why it was said. This is true in everyday life and this is true in the Bible.

---

[21] Although there is advantages to studying the original languages in which the Bible was written, the person who devotes himself to concentrated study of God's word often can handled the Word of God better than an "original language person" who does not have the same devotion.

One Monday morning a pastor received a forwarded email from a website with a copy of an article related to this sermon the day before. The identity of the person who initiated the sending of the article was not indicated. Consequently, the pastor was uncertain what the person was trying to say to him. Later, when the pastor learned the article was sent to him by someone trying to encouraging him, the article took on a completely different tone and meaning.

Absent knowing the motive/reason for something being said, the meaning is sometimes obscured and even understood to mean something very different than was intended by the author. Answering the question, "Why did the original author say that to the original audience?" is, for this reason, important to correct interpretation.

This second question is one of purpose and motivation in what was written. God, and the original author, had a purpose for writing what was written and recorded in the Bible. Identifying the purpose of the text is an important part of interpretation.

Thus the two gems produced as the fruit of careful interpretation are accurately identifying the meaning and the purpose of the passage. The meaning is <u>what</u> was said. The purpose is <u>why</u> it was said.

Using the book of Jude to illustrate:

- Jude 1:1-4 *WHAT: Jude wrote to encourage the believers to contend for the faith.*
  - WHY: Jude wanted the believer to be faithful and not follow false teachers.
- Jude 1:5-8 *WHAT: Jude told the believers that the condemnation of the false teachers is sure because it has been pronounced, demonstrated and meted out for the same offenses.*

- ○ WHY: Jude wanted believers to know that God will punish false teachers and is able to keep them faithful.

- Jude 1:8-16 *WHAT: Jude explained to the believers that the false teachers care only about themselves and are oblivious to their sure condemnation.*

  - ○ WHY: Jude wanted believers to understand the selfish nature of false teachers that brings condemnation on them.

- Jude 1:17-23 *WHAT: Jude told the believers to give care to their own relationship with the Lord and to help others with an attitude of mercy toward them.*

  - ○ WHY: Jude wanted the believers to show care and concern for people unlike the false teachers did.

- Jude 1:24-25 *WHAT: Jude told the believers that God is the one who is glorified, in everything He accomplishes in their lives.*

  - ○ WHY: Jude wanted the believers to understand God is able to keep them from being led astray by false teachers for His glory.

The results of interpretation form the basis for what the sermon will be about and why the sermon will be preached (or the lesson that will be taught).

- <u>What</u> God said in the *then and there* (interpretation) is the basis for

  - ○ <u>what</u> the preacher will say in the *here and now.* (application in sermon/lesson)

Likewise,

- <u>Why</u> God said what He said in the *then and there* (interpretation) becomes the basis for

- ○ <u>Why</u> the preacher will say what he does in the *here and now*. (application in sermon/lesson)

Although the sermon process includes a distinct transition from the *then and there* to the *here and now,* the meaning and purpose are retained as the basis for the sermon. By following this process it is ensured that the message of the Word of God is preserved and the preacher is God's messenger, not the message originator. When this process of careful interpretation is followed, the preacher can say with confidence "Thus says the Lord". Additionally, it will be obvious to those who hear the sermon that what is being said is clearly based on the Word of God. In the next section examples will be offered for how the transition from interpretation to application is made.

Chapter 7

Transitioning From Interpretation To Application
Preparing Sermons and Lessons based on the Bible Text

First the preacher must interpret the Scriptures and then he builds a sermon based upon the outcome of the careful and accurate interpretation process. At the end of interpretation, the preacher will have a clear understanding of the text consisting in two concise statements; one statement of the text meaning and the other statement of the text purpose. Both of these interpretative statements will be formed in terms of the original author and audience in the "then and there" setting of their time.

The transition to sermon/lesson preparation begins with a transformation of these two statements into parallel statements in terms of the modern audience. These two "here and now" statements become the sermon (homiletical idea) proposition and the sermon (homiletical) purpose.

A Practical Example from a New Testament Text

1 Peter 2:1-3 Therefore, putting aside all malice and all deceit and hypocrisy and envy and all slander, like newborn babies, long for the pure milk of the word, so that by it you may grow in respect to salvation, if you have tasted the kindness of the Lord.

The following illustrates how the results of interpretation are used to transition into preparing a Bible lesson or preparing a sermon.

A Text Outline based on a grammatical diagram would look something like this:

1. *You* long for the pure word that you may grow
   (a) laying aside
       i. all malice
       ii. all deceit
       iii. hypocrisy
       iv. envy
       v. all slander
   (b) as newborn infants long for milk
   (c) since you have tasted the kindness of the Lord

Text Interpretation (Historical - Then and There)	Application – Sermon or Lesson Preparation (Modern - Here and Now)
Text Main Idea: Peter tells/commands the Christians to long for the Word of God that they might grow in their salvation.	**Becomes Sermon Main Idea (proposition)** - God's Word is essential to your growth
Text Purpose: Peter wants to encourage the Christians to grow in the word.	**Becomes Sermon Purpose -** Encourage those present to long for God's Word that they might spiritually grow

Notice the correlation between the main idea of the text and the main idea/proposition of the sermon/lesson. Observe also the correspondence between the purpose of the text and the purpose of the sermon/lesson. Notice also that the sermon statements uses terms of application to the contemporary audience, "your growth". In this instance, there is almost a one to one relationship because the original audience was New Testament Christians and the modern audience (also New Testament Christians). The transition between interpretation and sermon building will not always be quite so parallel but there should always be a clear connection between the interpretation stage and the sermon building stage.

Similarly the main divisions in the sermon should arise from the text. Continuing with the example of 1 Peter 2:1-3 the main points of the sermon might be something like:

Text Relationship to . . . . Lesson/Sermon Main Points

Text says	Lesson/Sermon Main Points
Long for . . . *if you have tasted the kindness of the Lord*	Your appetite for the Word of God comes from experiencing the kindness of God – Salvation
Long for . . . *putting aside all malice . . .*	Your appetite for the Word of God requires spiritual exercise - Laying aside sin
Long for . . . *like newborn babies*	Your appetite for the Word of God should be satisfied by nothing else - humble and singular in focus

Notice the correlation between the main points in the sermon and the various aspects of the text. Observe also that the main points in the sermon are stated in terms of the particular audience who will hear the sermon. The main points do not directly mention the original audience nor the original author. Also, it can be seen that each of the main points in the sermon reinforce/explain the sermon proposition in some way. Each of the main points in the sermon also is consistent with, and serves to accomplish, the purpose of the sermon.

As previously described, the process of interpretation and sermon/lesson preparation can be illustrated with an hour glass. The top half of the hour glass is interpretation. The bottom half is sermon/lesson preparation. Just above the restricted neck of the hour glass is the text purpose and main idea and just below the restricted neck is the sermon/lesson purpose and sermon main idea. The sermon main idea is also called the sermon proposition, or simply the proposition. In the material that follows the terms sermon "main idea" and sermon "proposition" will be used interchangeably.

Typically the interpretation process will result in more facts, information and data than can ever be presented in the time allowed for a typical sermon. Consequently the teacher/preacher needs some means of determining what to include and what to exclude. Having determined the sermon purpose and proposition of the sermon the preacher then selects the material from the interpretation process needed to accomplish his purpose and to effectively communicate the proposition.

In a sense the sermon purpose and proposition form a grid through which the results of interpretation are screened for inclusion in the sermon. If something supports the proposition, and is consistent with the purpose then it is likely that it should be included. If something learned in the interpretation process does not both support the proposition and the purpose, then it should be excluded.

Unlike 1 Peter 2:1-3, other texts do not present such a nice and neat correlation between the interpretation process and the sermon development stage. New Testament teaching passages, especially the ones that deal with practical application, readily make the transition from interpretation to sermon/lesson preparation with minor differences. For some the transition consists of changing the terms from the then and there to the here and now. However, the same is not true in many other instances, including much of the Old Testament and narrative texts in the New Testament. The transition is also more difficult (and more critical) when dealing with passages that include narrative, figurative language, poetry, allegory, prophecy, etc.

An Old Testament Narrative Example

Joshua 1:2-3 "Moses My servant is dead; now therefore arise, cross this Jordan, you and all this people, to the land which I am giving to them, to the sons of Israel. "Every place on which the sole of your foot treads, I have given it to you, just as I spoke to Moses."

An outline of the text may look something like this:
1. God commanded Joshua to cross the Jordan
   (a) Moses is dead
   (b) along with all the people
   (c) to the land which God was giving them
2. God promised to give Joshua the land
   (a) every place the sole of his foot stepped
   (b) God had given it to Joshua
      i. just as he promised Moses.

Text Interpretation (Historical - Then and There)	Text Application Sermon or Lesson Preparation (Modern - Here and Now)
What? - God commanded Joshua to take possession of the land He had promised.	**Possible** Sermon (homiletical) proposition - God is faithful to His promises
Why? - to encourage Joshua to be obedient to enter the land	**Possible** Sermon (homiletical) Purpose - believers will be encouraged to be obedient to God because of God's faithfulness to His promises

The commands and promises to Joshua and Israel are not directly applicable to modern audiences and Christians today. Consequently there is a greater difference between the main idea of the text and the proposition of the sermon. However, there should be a clear and obvious correlation between the content of the text and the idea of the sermon. Many Bible texts are not directly applicable to Christians today. Thus it is even more critical to first correctly interpret and then, and only then, transition to sermon preparations. Much of the controversy and differences between churches and Christians would be readily eliminated if this method of interpretation was consistently practiced. Second to sinful pride, differences in interpretation practices is perhaps the greatest source of division among true Christians.

Failure to recognize that the promises regarding the land were made to Israel in interpretation may lead to many erroneous interpretations and corresponding sermons such as:

- God will give you all the land where you walk.

- You will be as powerful as Moses.

- Spiritualizing the text – Christian must march on Washington to change the nation.

It should be obvious that such sermons are not based on accurate interpretation. Equally obvious should be that without building the lesson/sermon on careful and accurate interpretation there is no limit to wild and crazy things a text can be made to say. In the absence of careful interpretation, the authority of the sermon/lesson resides neither with God, nor with the Bible, but with the preacher. This is not a good thing and is the source of many bad sermons, no matter how many accolades a preacher may receive.

When the interpretive work is done and the transition to sermon preparation has identified the sermon purpose and sermon proposition, then the preacher needs to take steps to ensure that the sermon itself will be cohesive. This cohesiveness has been alluded to already with the mention of a grid that provides a screen for what is included and what is excluded in the sermon itself.

Chapter 8

Selecting And "CULLING" Sermon Content

As mentioned at the beginning, for the teacher or preacher of God's Word to be effective there are two things that are essential. The preacher must:

1. have something worthwhile to say, and
2. be able to communicate effectively

So far the primary focus has been on performing the background work of interpretation necessary for preparing a sermon/lesson to present. Repeatedly it has been emphasized that a good sermon is founded upon good interpretation. The preacher or teacher who prepares by careful interpretation followed by purposeful transitions will have something worthwhile to say – God's Word, and not just some preacher's opinion.

There are many other aspects to interpretation that could be addressed. These may include doing word studies, using Bible Dictionaries, lexicons, Bible Encyclopedias, cross references and commentaries. All of these have a place and role in interpretation. It would be good to become proficient in all of these. However, there is no substitute for concentrated focus and time spent reading the Bible broadly and studying the text intensely.

In this chapter, and the next few chapters, the focus will be on the lower half of the hour glass of sermon preparation. The top half of the hour glass is the interpretation process. Interpretation is completed with stating concise summaries the text's main idea and the text's purpose as intended by the original author. The transition to sermon preparation keeps the products of interpretation as a basis for content and purpose of the sermon. Thus the bottom half of the hour glass is sermon/lesson preparation that begins with formulating statements of the sermon purpose and the sermon proposition derived from the results and products of interpretation.

In a sense, the sermon purpose and the sermon proposition are like the two rails of the train track upon which the sermon itself will travel. They also serve as the screen through which everything in the sermon must pass in order to be included.

As mentioned before, the interpretation process almost always yields much more information (word meanings, historical facts, cross references, potential illustrations and applications, etc) than there will be time available to communicate. It is as if the preacher has filled a ten-yard dump truck with material to deliver but is given little Toyota pickup worth of time in which to deliver it.

The abundance of material requires the preacher to determine some effective way to prepare a sermon that is both faithful to God's Word and still meets the external constraints of time limits that are imposed. Fortunately, if the transition from interpretation to sermon preparation has been done well, much of the work of figuring out what to include and what to exclude is already complete.

A sermon purpose and proposition based squarely upon the text serve as the screening criteria for what goes into the sermon and what is omitted. That which accomplishes the sermon purpose and communicates the sermon proposition is included.

That which does not serve to accomplish the purpose or to communicate the sermon proposition is excluded.

In other words, the proposition of the sermon is the one thing which the preacher wants the people to take home from the sermon. When asked, "What was the sermon about?" every listener should respond with some form of restatement of the proposition of the sermon. The sermon is like a hammer that pounds the nail of the sermon proposition into the head of the hearer. The sermon can be likened to a screwdriver which twists the screw of the proposition into the heart of God's people.

Thus, everything under consideration for inclusion in the sermon is put to these tests:

1. Does it help accomplish the purpose of the sermon? and,

2. Does it help communicate the proposition?

If the answer to either question is "no" then it should not be in the sermon no matter how interesting, intriguing, informative or funny it may be. If the "answer" to both questions is "yes" then it is likely that it should be included in the sermon, at least in the first draft. Unfortunately, there is usually more that does meet both the criteria than there is time, and much of the "good stuff" must be excluded to include the "best stuff".

Even when a preacher takes care to ensure that only the best material is retained in the sermon, everyone knows that the preacher is likely to go over-time 9 out of 10 times and that he never finishes early. What is not obvious to everyone though is that most preachers are leaving out and skipping over information in their notes in the course of preaching the sermon. Deciding what to leave out while preaching is difficult. It is hard to deliver a coherent message if one is having to select and omit material "on the fly". It is much better to plan well and then to preach the sermon as planned. The starting point for limiting material for the sermon is to only include what accomplishes the purpose and communicates the proposition.

Limiting sermon content is important regarding time but it is even more vital for the sake of the cohesiveness of the sermon. Some sermons are like the pattern made by a shot-gun at 300 yards. The sermon makes a lot of noise and smoke but lacks impact because the sermon is spread all over rather than carefully aimed like a high powered rifle. By having a specific purpose and a specific proposition for each sermon, the preacher has a clearly defined target at which to aim. Every word that is spoken becomes like another grain of powder in the rifle shell to ensure that the target is hit, hit accurately and hit with adequate force. The right target of course is identified by interpreting the passage.

Ideally, if those leaving the church were asked "What did the preacher say?" they should reply by stating the proposition in some recognizable form. If those same people were asked, "What was the preacher trying to accomplish today?" ideally they would state the sermon purpose in some way.

Another aspect of this screening grid to provide sermon unity is the careful selection of a connective word that describes all the main points of the sermon.

Chapter 9

Choosing A Connecting Word
(think shooting with a rifle at a target rather than a shotgun)

A sermon should be a single message with a single purpose, aimed at those who listen.

To achieve this degree of unity in the the sermon the preacher clearly identifies the sermon purpose and sermon proposition – both derived from the careful interpretation of the sermon text.

Another means of attaining unity in the sermon is to select a connecting word that describes each major division of the sermon and also helps organize the sermon so people can comprehend what is being said. The connecting word provides additional cohesiveness to the sermon and increases the likelihood that the audience will comprehend the message.

A Connecting Word is:
1. a plural noun that describes each of the main points of the sermon.
2. often used in transition sentences between major parts of the sermon
3. a means of unifying the sermon for ease of preaching
4. a means of unifying the sermon for ease of hearing, understanding and implementing.

Consideration of the below examples (and those in Appendix C) will illustrate the role and value of a carefully chosen Connecting Word.

Text: 1 Peter 1:3-5
Proposition: We bless God who has given us new life. . . . .
    (Single Message of the Sermon)
Purpose: Believers will worship God. . . . .
    (Single Purpose of the Sermon)
Connecting Word: **Reasons** . . (Word that describes each main point)
Sermon Outline with Main Points

Proposition: **We bless God who has given us new life . . .**
. . . BECAUSE (reason #1)
   1. God has caused us to be born again
. . . BECAUSE (reason #2)
   2. Our new life is by God's Mercy
. . . BECAUSE (reason #3)
   3. Our new life produces an undying hope
. . . BECAUSE (reason #4)
   4. Our new life was accomplished by Jesus resurrection from the dead
. . . BECAUSE (reason#5)
   5. Our new life is protected by the power of God

   NOTE: Each point in the sermon outline is a **reason** (connecting word) that emphasizes the sermon proposition and accomplishes the sermon purpose.

   We Bless God who has given us new life (proposition) – reason #1 God has caused us to be born again; Reason #2 Our new life is because of God's mercy . . . . #3, #4, #5.

   The emphasis on the word "because" is used in this example to show the relationship between the proposistion, the main points and the connecting word.

   We bless God who has given us new life! Why? The main points are the reasons we bless God . . . We bless God "because . . . (five reasons).

Text: 1 Pet 1:13-16
Proposition: When your hope is in God then there will be holiness in your life.

Purpose: The believers will fully hope in God so that they may be holy.

Connecting Word: **Characteristics**

    (Characteristics of one with hope in God that will live a holy life)

Sermon Outline with Main Points

Characteristic #1 (of the one with hope in God who will live holy)
1. Our hope is to be exclusively place on God's grace.

Characteristic #2 (of the one with hope in God who will live holy)
2. Personal holiness is expected of all the children of God.

Text: 1 Pet 1:22-25

Proposition: Loving people is made possible by God.
Purpose: People will be encouraged to love one another
Connecting Word: **Provisions**

Sermon Outline with Main Points
    (each point is a <u>provision</u> made possible by God to love people)
1. Loving people is based on salvation
2. Loving people is based on God's love
3. Loving people is based on understanding what is eternal.

A review of each of the above examples demonstrate how each sermon is a cohesive unit.
- In 1 Pet 1:3-5 are five <u>reasons</u> why "We bless God who has given us new life."
- In 1 Peter 1:13-16 there are two <u>Characteristics</u> of Christians.

- In 1 Peter 1:22-25 there are three <u>provisions</u> from God for loving people.

Notice that the connecting word ties each of the main points of each sermon to the proposition of that sermon. The connecting words also helps people to listen and to track with the sermon. Sermons are easier to follow and understand if there is unity in the message. If easier to understand, then it is easier to put into practice. Thus, having a connecting word is a very helpful tool in sermon preparation and delivery from the perspective of the audience.

A sermon that is linked together by a connecting word is also easier for the preacher. It is easier for him to remember what he plans to say and therefore easier to preach. Ease in preaching comes from the sermon being a single unit rather than a random collection of ideas. Constructed in this way, the preacher can fully grasp the sermon proposition, the sermon purpose and the connecting word that ties the main points together. The sermon *almost* preaches itself because the preacher has done the work necessary to personally grasp the content of the sermon himself before attempting to communicate it.

Although there are many approaches to sermon constructions, this suggested method provides a consistent and very helpful format that is highly recommended for adoption until the preacher becomes proficient. After proficiency is attained in preparing and preaching sound Bibilical sermons there are many variations that can be effectively utilized to communicate God's truth.

Preparing and preaching sermons requires great care and effort by the preacher. However both understanding and communicating the truth of God is a spiritual endeavor that the preacher cannot effectively accomplish by his own intellect nor in his own strength. The preacher must put forth 100% effort, but also must prayerfully rely upon God to guide him at every step of the way.

Chapter 10

Hard Work <u>and</u> the Holy Spirit

There has been an unspoken assumption behind all that has been said up to this point. The one preparing to teach or preach will bathe the entire process in prayer in dependence on the Holy Spirit.

Admittedly, there has been a significant emphasis on the hard work, study and effort by the preacher to prepare a sermon. However, all of the preacher's efforts are to be done with a dependence on God. God enables accurate interpretation, gives wisdom in constructing the sermon, provides power in preaching and accomplishes the work in people's hearts who hear the sermon. At each stage the preacher should recognize his own limitations, acknowledge them to God and ask God to accomplish His work in the preacher and in those who will eventually hear the sermon.

The strong emphasis in earlier chapters on the preacher's need to be careful in interpretation and diligent in studying may lead some to think that the task can be done through human effort. Contrary to such a conclusion, dependence on God is essential.
There are two kinds of preachers that need to be reminded that preaching is only effective if God is at work:

- those who have been preaching more than two years **and**

- those who have been preaching less than two years.

Preachers who are fairly new at preaching often have a tendency to work so hard that they think that they have a handle on it and forget to call upon God to work first in them and then in the people. Preachers who have been preaching for many years are practiced and polished and may tend to think that they could preach in their sleep. The reality is that if God is not in every step of the process the preacher and people would do just as well to sit in church and stare at the wall for an hour.

Preachers need to take time apart to pray before sharing God's Word because unless they are abiding in Jesus they can accomplish nothing.[22] The effectiveness of the sermon in the life of people depends on God working in their hearts. Preachers should acknowledge God's sovereignty in their preaching as well as all areas of life. Preachers need to see both their responsibilities and God's sovereignty within the same picture frame. Embracing and maintaining this balance has within it some obvious inherent tensions. But these tensions should be allowed to exist without going to one end of the spectrum or the other.

It is helpful for the preacher to consider the following regarding these seemingly incompatible perspectives.

- 100 % - First, the preacher should prepare as if it all depends on him, **because it does.**
  - If the preacher does not work hard then the outcome will be less than what it should be. Slip-shod interpretation, disconnected thoughts, poor delivery, etc. are some of the signs that the preacher has not done his homework diligently.
- 100 % - Second, the preacher should pray as if it all depends on God, **because it does.**
  - If God does not open the preacher's mind to understand His word, he cannot prepare a good sermon.

---

22   John 15:5 "I am the vine, you are the branches; he who abides in Me and I in him, he bears much fruit, for apart from Me you can do nothing.

- ○ If God does not empower the preaching of the word, then it will be ineffective in its delivery.

- ○ If God does not open the hearts of the people, no matter how good the sermon may have been, it is worthless.

- 100 % - Third, the preacher preaches as if it all depends on those hearing the message, **because it does.**

  - ○ If the Word of God is presented in a faithful, accurate and applicable way, then it is the hearer's responsibility to put it into practice.

  - ○ When it comes to delivering the message, the one hearing should feel the responsibility to be doers of the word and not hearers only.

Accordingly, 300% is required for the preaching of God's Word to accomplish its purposes in the life of a person. Although 300% may not make sense in an earthly realm, sermon preparation and preaching is a spiritual endeavor and the math makes perfect sense.

Each step of the process - interpretation, sermon preparation and preaching - depends on God and the teacher/preacher. Thus prayer and dependence on the Holy Spirit is essential. Admittedly, God may still work if we fall short, but in such cases He works despite us, rather than because of us.

Chapter 11

Illustrations

Some preachers find a good joke and then pray, "Father, I ask that you give me a good text to accompany this fantastic joke." They have something funny they want to say and then try to build the sermon around this.

Of course, as has been previously discussed, sermons should be based upon the text, not the text based upon the joke or story.

However, there is a place for jokes and stories in sermons, but how they are used is very important.

It would be a wonderful thing if the teacher or preacher could simply explain what God says and expect that each one would carefully listen, take it to heart and make the appropriate adjustments in their lives. If this were to happen, there would be much more spiritual growth occurring within the church. Yet, people are not necessarily inclined to listen. It is hard for most people to listen for long. Even when they hear, they often do not care enough to take it to heart and actually change.

As stated before, effective preaching requires two essential things.

1. The preacher must have something worthwhile to say, and

2. The preacher must be able to communicate it effectively

Illustrations are one tool to facilitate effective communication of the truth. Although communicating the truth should be simple after it is understood, it actually is a rather formidable undertaking.

Communication of the truth of God's Word has been effective when those who are hearing the sermon understand that same truth themselves.

Striving to be effective in communication is part of the reason for identifying a precise statement of the <u>sermon proposition</u> and <u>sermon purpose</u>. These statements help the preacher to know exactly what he is trying to say and why he is saying it. (Remember, the proposition is that one truth the preacher intends the hearer to leave with.) The <u>connecting word</u> ties the sermon together. The <u>outline</u> gives structure to the message so that each major point of the outline serves to accomplish the purpose of the sermon and emphasizes some aspect of the proposition. All of these contribute to the unity of the message to facilitate effective communication.

Yet there is still more that can be done to effectively communicate. Communication is most effective when 1) people can relate to what is being said and 2) people understand how to put into practice what is being said. Illustrations help people relate to what is being said. Applications help people put God's truth into practice.

The addition of appropriate illustrations and applications to a sermon will make it easier for people to listen and to put the truth into practice. Illustrations and applications should be added to the sermon <u>after</u> the main structure of the sermon is in place including proposition, purpose, connecting word, main points and sub-points.

Illustrations are examples given to aid in understanding. One writer has described illustrations as "raisins in the oatmeal." They are tasty and interesting morsels in the midst of what might be otherwise boring or unpalatable. Illustrations can take many forms. Object lessons, skits, pictures, stories, anecdotes, etc. can be effectively used to emphasize a point. The most common type of illustration used in preaching is a word picture. The preacher tells a story, relates an

incident, shares a happening, gives some statistics, reads from a
newspaper, or tells a joke that paints a picture in the mind of the hearer
that enhances understanding of what is being said.

Illustrations also facilitate remembering what was said. Many church
goers can readily repeat the story or joke but don't remember much
else from the sermon. Using illustrations that helps listener to
understand and remember the truth of God is the goal of the preacher.
If the hearer laughs at a humorous illustration, it personalizes the truth.
If an illustration arouses emotions, people are hearing the Word with
their hearts as wells as their ears.

The preacher must always be aware that illustrations are a means to an
end. Illustrations should be carefully selected to accomplish the
intended goal. The goal of the sermon is to accomplish the sermon
purpose and to communicate the proposition of the sermon. Just as the
biblical content of the sermon is screened and selected by the sermon
purpose and proposition, so are illustrations. When considering
illustrations, there are several "screening" questions that must be
asked:

- Does the illustration help accomplish the sermon purpose? (if
  "no" then leave it out)

- Does the illustration help illustrate the point being made? (if
  "no" then leave it out)

- Is the illustration appropriate for those listening? (if "no" then
  leave it out)

- Is this the best illustration available for making the point? (if
  "no" then leave it out)

Illustrations are a very valuable and powerful communication tool.
They can change an otherwise mundane and mediocre sermon into a
life changing experience. It is true that the Word of God changes lives
by the power of God's Spirit working within the individual. However,

illustrations are one of the tools which God has given to communicate His Word to the heart of people. Jesus was a master of illustrations, painting word pictures from common life to reinforce spiritual truth:

- . . . "a sower went out to sow"
- . . . "look at the lilies of the field"
- . . . "I am the true vine"
- . . . "the fields are ripe for harvest"
- . . . "the kingdom of heaven is like"
- . . . "you are whitewashed tombs"

God's Word is so precious and exciting. Preachers do everyone a great disservice when they present the Word in such a way that seems boring and spawns disinterest. Although it is God's job to work in people's hearts, it is the preacher's task to do all that he can so that the Word is heard. Illustrations are one method that can be used to connect the truth of God to the lives of those who hear.

How many illustrations should there be in a sermon? A general guideline is that each main point in the outline should have at least one illustration. Three points - three illustrations; Four points - four illustrations, etc. While this may serve as a basic rule, it is better to ask, how many illustrations are needed and appropriate. Time is always a factor too. One can spend too much time on illustrations and fail to give appropriate attention to the truth of God. The length of the illustration is a factor as well. Longer illustrations mean fewer can be used. On the other hand a number of "one-liners" may be used together.

Illustrations can be found in many ways. One of the best sources of illustrations is daily life including those things encountered by people anywhere and everywhere. The key to identifying illustrations is to be looking for them. Although illustrations are not selected for addition to the sermon until the main components are in place, it is completely appropriate, even helpful, to be gathering potential sermon illustrations during the interpretation and sermon construction process.

It is quite natural for the preacher to think of applications and illustrations while studying and meditating upon a text of Scripture. During all stages of studying and sermon preparation the preacher can identify and record them for <u>possible</u> inclusion in the sermon when the time comes.[23] Observing people, reading the newspaper, animal behavior . . . everything offers a source of potential sermon illustration. When something may potentially serve as a good illustration, it can be recorded by a few words for later consideration. After the sermon is structured, the preacher can review potential illustration to determine if they will serve the sermon well or not. This judgment cannot be made until the preacher knows the sermon proposition, purpose, connecting word and main points as a minimum.

The sermon is about communicating God's Word. Illustrations are simply one tool that can be used to enhance effective communication. If an illustration does not help reach the goal, it should be omitted. No matter how funny a joke may be, it should not be used if it does not serve to communicate the proposition or one of the main points. Although a morsel of God's word, and a truck load of illustrations may make for a lively, humorous and interesting sermon, preachers must always remember that they are called on to "preach the **WORD**" because it is God's Words that will change people's lives.

It serves the preacher well to always remember these warning and instructions:

> I solemnly charge *you* in the presence of God and of Christ
> Jesus, who is to judge the living and the dead, and by His

---

[23] The author records all the illustrations and applications that come to mind indiscriminately during all the phases of the interpretation and sermon preparation. After the message content and structure of the sermon is formed based on the text, he then selects appropriate illustrations for inclusion. Those that do not fit are left out.

appearing and His kingdom: <u>preach the word</u>; be ready in season *and* out of season; reprove, rebuke, exhort, with great patience and instruction. For the time will come when they will not endure sound doctrine; but *wanting* to have their ears tickled, they will accumulate for themselves teachers in accordance to their own desires, and will turn away their ears from the truth and will turn aside to myths. 2 Timothy 4:1-4

Chapter 12

Applications

According to the teaching of James, the brother of Jesus, those who hear the Word of God are to put it into practice. Preachers who include applications in their lessons/sermons are helping people to become "doers of the Word and not merely hearers who delude themselves." (James 1:22)

Previously, a careful distinction was made between interpretation and application. Interpretation is identifying the text's main idea and purpose in terms of the original audience at the time and place where it was said. When the transition is made to sermon preparation, the preacher crosses the bridge into the "here and now" bringing along with him the products of interpretation. Sermon preparation involves applying the truths of Scripture to the modern audience. The sermon purpose and proposition are stated in terms of application relating to what the modern hearer is to do in response to what God's Word said.

Unless it is clearly understood how to put the truth of scripture in one's life how will they be able to be doers of the word? Application is essential if one is going to obey God in of faith and love in deed and not in word only.[24] Application answers the questions regarding what the Scriptures says. Questions like:

- "So What?" and
- "What does the Scripture say (or mean) **to me**?"
- What should I do and how do I do that?

---

[24]   1 John 3:18 Little children, let us not love with word or with tongue, but in deed and truth.

Although seeking answers to these questions during interpretation may be a hindrance to accurate interpretation, during sermon preparation they are essential and people need the answers. Interpretation without application leaves a sermon potentially sterile and ineffective in people's lives.

Although the sermon focuses on application in general, it is very helpful to include specific applications to help people know how to respond to the message of the sermon. Applications in preaching are suggestions offered as ways of putting into practice what the Bible says.

Although there is usually one, and only one, correct interpretation of a given text, there can be many appropriate applications. Although the interpretation is rooted firmly in the text, appropriate application depends largely upon the needs of the audience. When applications are used in preaching it is like the preacher dipping the paint brush into the can, drawing attention to the paint and applying a few strokes to the wall. *(Notice that is an illustration)* Applications are the "how to's" of doing what the Word of God says. Some sermon texts are very practical and directly apply to people's lives. For these texts applications are found in, or very close to exactly what the text is saying. Other portions of Scripture deal with issues that are a bit more theoretical or philosophical (sovereignty of God, holiness, narrative passages, etc.) and therefore require more effort to ensure that those hearing should understand **what** they should do in response to what the Bible says.

For example, a sermon from Jude 1:3-4 may have as a proposition, "You should contend for the faith". Applications for this sermon may included:

- describing a program of Bible reading.
- explaining how to becoming discerning about truth.

- encouraging and explaining how to confront of error.
- describing how to conduct church discipline processes.
- describing how to repent of sin to be spiritually sensitive.

Illustrations aid in understanding and remembering the Scriptures. Applications aid in putting into practice the Scriptures. A single story may contain both an application and illustration.

How many applications should be given? The same suggestions offered for illustrations can be made for applications. At least one per main outline point. The same type of questions for limiting illustrations also applies regarding appropriateness of applications for inclusion.

Illustrations are like salt and applications like pepper. They are to be used to bring out the flavor of God's Word so that the people will long for it. But to make a meal of either one is not very palatable and certainly would not be pleasing to God. *(Notice the illustration)* The admonition of *Colossians 4:6 (Let your speech always be with grace, as though seasoned with salt, so that you will know how you should respond to each person.)* says to choose words for the impact they will have. This certainly applies to the preacher and his sermon.

Illustrations and applications often have a special role in sermon introductions and conclusions which will be considered in the next chapter.

Chapter 13

Introductions, Conclusions and Transitions

The last two chapters discussed Illustrations and Applications as a way of keeping the attention of those who hear the sermon and helping them to put God's word into practice in their lives. Also it was mentioned that illustrations help drive home the point being made in the sermon so people have some handles that they can grab. Similarly, the sermon introduction is intended to connect the sermon to the audience.

The <u>Introduction</u> of a sermon is intended to capture the attention of the people and to lead their thinking in the direction of the subject at hand. Every sermon benefits from an introduction. The introduction may be short and simple or long and complex. Either way it serves the important function of introducing the audience to the subject of the sermon.

Following are some ideas which may be used to introduce the sermon:

- Read a text, ask a question about it, or make a statement regarding it.
- Offer some statistics - "1 out of 2 kids live in single parent homes."
- Make an unusual statement - "The Bible says there is no God!"
- Present a problem - "What do you do when God seems not to hear your prayers?"
- Tell a story - tell of a life situation, real or fictitious
- Present a joke - humor related to the message

-
- State the purpose - "Today we are going to learn how God views homosexuality"
- Ask a Question - "Have you ever . . .?" "Did you know . . .?" "How many times . . .?"
- Explain a life situation - describe an incident or happening

Good Introductions:

- Present a thought related to the proposition of the sermon

- Generally consist of a single thought rather than a number of thoughts

- Are specific in nature rather than broad and general.

- Do not promise more than can be delivered in the sermon

- Are simple, but carefully prepared.

- As a rule, short is usually better; time is a premium.

The conclusion of the sermon is also important. Sometimes sermons just taper off and fade away. Other times they end so abruptly that people are left wondering if the preacher was called to an emergency in the middle of preparing and did not have time to finish. As with the introduction, the conclusion is a needful and important part of the sermon. Below are several suggestions for methods of concluding the sermon.

- Review the main points of the message.

- Make application - giving advice or counsel how people may practice the message preached.

- Make appeal - Ask the people to do something; gospel invitation.

- Encourage or Warn.

- Use an illustration to summarize the proposition of the message.

- Read and emphasize significant words in the text.

<u>Some guidelines for a conclusion.</u> The conclusion should:

- Be prepared in advance, but able to be modified depending on the Spirit's leading.
- Actually conclude the message.
- <u>Not</u> introduce new material or ideas
- Focus on the hearers with a view to application
- Usually should end the message on a positive note.

A third area of sermon preparation worthy of mention is planning ahead for purposeful transitions. The sermon usually consists of several different parts that, although related, are also different and distinct. The parts of the sermon usually consist of an introduction, several main points and a conclusion. Transitions are the bridges that span from one part to another. In most cases the transition is made with a single sentence which links the two sections together smoothly rather than abruptly "changing the subject."

It is often highly advisable for each transition sentence (TS) to be fully written out in the sermon outline. A transition sentence should be used between the introduction and the sermon body, between the sections of the sermon body and between the sermon body and the conclusion.

Carefully crafted transition sentences can also serve to help present the sermon in as a single unit by using the sermon "connecting word" in the sentence. For example, if the connecting word in the sermon is "essentials" then it is quite natural that the transition sentences utilize that word. (Remember the connecting word is a single word that describes all of the main points in the sermon outline.) So after the introduction the transition sentence might be: "*The first **essential** for being a good father is to be a good follower of Jesus.*" A transition from the third point to the conclusion might be "*So you see in today's text three **essentials** for being a good father.*" The conclusion then could review each essential and challenge the fathers to put them into practice.

There is another transition in preaching a sermon that deserves special attention - but it is not a transition in the technical sense. Rather it is the first thing that the preacher says as part of the sermon. This could be called the "Approach Sentence" (AS). The first words from the preacher's mouth can make or break the sermon. Like transition sentences, it is helpful to prepare and write out the approach sentence. Writing out approach and transition sentences helps the hearers to track with the transitions and also reminds the preacher where he has been and where he is headed.

Introductions, conclusions and transitions are important in sermons because they help the preacher communicate the Word of God effectively.

Chapter 14

Delivery - Preaching a Sermon

The Apostle Paul wrote to the church at Corinth and said,

> *"And when I came to you, brethren, I did not come with superiority of speech or of wisdom, proclaiming to you the testimony of God. For I determined to know nothing among you except Jesus Christ, and Him crucified. I was with you in weakness and in fear and in much trembling, and my message and my preaching were not in persuasive words of wisdom, but in demonstration of the Spirit and of power, so that your faith would not rest on the wisdom of men, but on the power of God."* 1 Corinthians 2:1-4

These are important words for those who preach the Word of God. It is not the charisma of the preacher nor the eloquence of his words that bring people to the Lord.

> **Effective sermons depend on the <u>power</u> of God found in the <u>message</u> of God delivered by the <u>man</u> of God depending on the <u>Spirit</u> of God.**

However, this is not saying that preaching should be without preparation or thought of what will be said and how it will be said. Laziness often wears the thin veneer of being spiritual. "Being led by the Spirit" can become an excuse for not studying and for not preparing words carefully before hand. It is important to be "led by the Spirit" but it is also important to prepare in the power of the Spirit. Being an effective communicator does not come naturally for most. Thus it is very important for the preacher to learn how to communicate well. Poorly communicating the best sermon in the world makes for a poor sermon.

Whole volumes have been written on preaching and sermon delivery. Many of them are valuable and helpful. Following are a few pointers and a few common pitfalls that speakers often encounter.

Speak clearly – form words carefully and enunciate clearly. Be careful not to mumble or speak in garbled language. Speakers, especially those who are inexperienced, have a tendency to speak too rapidly and try to hurry through what they are trying to say. It is much better to carefully say each word so that people can hear it than to speak so quickly that the sounds of the words run together and are indiscernible.

Vary speaking tone - monotone speaking is boring even if the subject matter is very exciting. Changing the pitch of words, and the pitch pattern of sentences will be helpful in keeping people's interest.

Vary speaking speed - It is a good effect to sometimes speak slowly, even very slowly or to speak rapidly, even very rapidly (as long as the word can be understood). Sometimes it is good to even stop talking for a few seconds - a long pause can sometimes be more effective than a bucket full of words.

Vary volume - From whispering to yelling, a speaker can and should vary the volume of his voice. A hushed voice can make a point better than screaming. People will listen as if you are telling a secret. An elevated voice will capture their attention but will soon become irritating if used to excess.

Note: Speaking variations are changing from the norm. If the norm is constant variation then there is no norm and the benefit of including variation is lost. Variation should be used to emphasize a point, to recapture the peoples' attention, to wake somebody up, to express strong emotion, etc.

Gesture freely - Don't be a statue. Move around a bit. Move your hands and arms. Use facial expression. Communication is accomplished with much more than words. Smile when speaking of joy and make a face showing disgust when speaking of something disgusting.

Speak to the people, not the wall, ceiling or pulpit - when speaking people want to know and feel that you are talking to them, not delivering some speech. Avoid the tendency to look at something other than the people. Make eye contact with different people as you speak. Be careful not to look at just one person or group of people for this will alienate others and perhaps needlessly offend those in whose direction you make all you comments. Look around the room in a smooth way to include all the people.

Be Real - Do not try to be like some big name popular preacher (or your own pastor). Be yourself. Use your own vocabulary, your own mannerism and your own style. Do not put on a preaching voice, preaching gestures, preaching clothes or preaching posture. People want to hear what the Lord has to say from your heart in your way.

Show appropriate enthusiasm - Know your message, believe your message and communicate your message. The preacher who does not care what the Lord has said cannot expect the people to care. People will sense when the preacher is just going through the motions and will tend not to listen. Although the message is from the Lord, at some point, and in some way the message becomes the preacher's. He should speak it with conviction and enthusiasm.

Avoid distracting mannerism - If the preacher has a habit that distracts from the people hearing the message it needs to be changed.

There are obvious things to avoid such as picking your nose, scratching in inappropriate places, and jingling pocket change/keys. Other things are less obvious but often just as detrimental.

Avoid slang - although people may use slang in daily conversations it usually is inappropriate in the pulpit. Some may not mind it, but others will be offended and be distracted by it. (It should not need to be said, but it does need to be said – do not use profanity.)

Avoid "pause words" - when the preacher is trying to gather his thoughts he does not need to say anything. Do not fill the blank time with non-words such as "uuuuuuuuuhhhhhhh," "aaaaaannnnnndddddd," "ooooookkkaaaayyyyy" and the like. (People may even begin to count how many times you say these words rather than listen to what is being said.)

Love the people. Don't be constantly spanking them. Preachers who are constantly dealing with God's word and with sinning people tend to take the opportunity in the pulpit what they are too timid to do in person. Avoid the temptation to hide behind the pulpit to always chastise the people. The Word of God indeed has a reproving aspect and God does desire us all to change. But the preacher who constantly cracks the whip is wearying. Rather, try to be an encouragement to the people. Show them that you have love and compassion for them. Often this is not so much what you say, but how you say it. It includes posture, tone, facial expression etc.

Do not demean yourself - Although you may not have great confidence in your ability to speak, do not downgrade yourself verbally before the people. Do not make excuses such as not being polished, not being prepared, not being practiced etc. To demean yourself simply draws attention to yourself and distracts from the Lord and from the message. It is good to be humble but it is not good to parade your deficiencies (false humility)[25] before the people. They will perceive them well enough and to draw attention to such does no good.

Say it and then stop - Do not think that you have to fill the time slot. When you have said what you came to say - stop. Even if you are 20 minutes early - once the truck is unloaded, do not keep banging the shovel against the bed just to fill the time. (*notice the illustration*) Say it! Commit it to the Lord! And Sit Down! To keep going when you are just filling the time is like watering down juice. Pretty soon people tire and the juice loses its flavor.

Practice the Sermon - It is difficult to judge how the sermon will flow, how it will sound, how it will come across until it is verbalized. Practicing also provides a measure of the length of the sermon. Here are a few thing preachers sometimes do to practice.

> Practice out loud. Practice in private. Practice before a mirror (some find this distracting but others find it helpful). Practice while video taping and then review. Practice before others who will be gentle but will also give helpful suggestions.

Learning to be effective in sermon delivery is often enhanced by having a loving and gentle, but honest friend who will identify things that distract and can be done better in sermon delivery. Appendix E has been provided as a guide for sermon evaluations. Seeking out such a brother (or wife) can provide much assistance in improving in this area. These are a few things that will aid in effectively delivering the sermon.

---

[25] Parading one's deficiencies is a false humility because it focuses attention on yourself, which is actually a form of pride.

Chapter 15

To Preach or Not to Preach?

It is commonly held that people's greatest fear is "public speaking."
Few would deny that preaching a sermon qualifies as public
speaking. So it is not surprising that there is often an apprehension
associated with stepping into the pulpit. This universal fear,
combined with a healthy respect for God, His Word and the great
responsibility associated with preaching, may lead to the
conclusion that only presumptuous arrogant fools would ever
preach.

Admittedly for some, preaching and being in the limelight is a
matter of pride. However, pride also plays a part in keeping men
out of the pulpit. Preaching, and doing it well, is a very humbling
thing and most men do not want to be either humbled or
humiliated. So how does pride keep men from preaching, speaking
publicly?

- Fear of Public Speaking: Do people really fear public
  speaking or is there some other fear beneath the surface?
  Many answers may be offered to the question "Why do
  people fear public speaking?" But most of the answers
  come down to this - people are afraid of being humbled or
  humiliated in the eyes of others. No one wants to "look
  bad." No one wants a whole group of people to think bad
  of them. So people "fear" putting themselves in a situation
  where everyone is staring at them, is evaluating every word
  and potentially forming an unfavorable opinion about them.

- Pride is often one source, if not the primary source of the fear of public speaking.

There are other reasons some decline opportunities to preach.

- Fear of wrongly handling the Word of God: The one who does not acknowledge that preaching is a weighty responsibility should certainly never presume to step behind a pulpit to preach, nor be allowed to do so. However, the weight of that responsibility should not keep anyone from preaching. Rather, the gravity of the task should stimulate diligence and careful study. It is every Christian's responsibility to study the Word of God, to understand the Word of God and to share the Word of God. Preaching accomplishes all of these. The responsibility associated with preaching causes individuals to see their own deficiencies in their responsibility to study God's Word. Rather than fix the deficiency some choose not to be obedient to the Lord.

- Priorities - Preparation to preach takes a lot of time and effort. Preparation to preach well takes more time and effort. Some men are unwilling to devote the time needed to prepare and preach sermons. But, really, what is more important than breaking the bread of life so that people will come to know the Savior and grow by His grace?

Those who are committed to be obedient to the Lord will humble themselves before God and faithfully speak the Word of God as opportunities arise. The opportunity to preach or teach God's Word should be embraced. Fear of public speaking is pride that should never keep one from faithfulness to God.

The things which you have heard from me in the presence of many witnesses, entrust these to faithful men who will be able to teach others also. 2 Timothy 2:2

Appendix A: Interpretation Worksheet Template

A template like this may be helpful for recording observations, questions, comments, potential sermon illustrations/applications. An electronic copy of the template can be used and then filled in while studying and interpreting the text.

Text: _____ Date: _____ Pray

1. Comments on reading
   (a)
   (b)
   (c)
2. Potential ILLUSTRATIONS
   (a)
   (b)
   (c)
3. Potential APPLICATIONS
   (a)
   (b)
   (c)
4. Comments on diagram and grammar
   (a)
   (b)
   (c)
5. Word Studies

6. CROSS REFERENCES

7. Exegetical (Interpretation)Outline
   (a) Exegetical idea
   (b) Exegetical Purpose

8. Sermonic (Preaching or Lesson) Process
   (a) Sermon purpose
   (b) Sermon Main Idea (Proposition)
9. Choose the Connecting Word

Appendix B: Sermon Preparation Template

A template like this can be helpful to organize the sermon and help remember the important components of the sermon

Text:
Title:
PURPOSE:
PROPOSITION (Main Idea):
Connecting word -

A.S./T.S. (approach sentence/Transition Sentence)
Intro:
T.S.(Includes Connecting Word)
   1.
      (a)
      (b)
      (c)
      (d)
Illustration/Application?
T.S. (Includes Connecting Word)
   2.
      (a)
      (b)
      (c)
      (d)
Illustration/Application?
T.S.(Includes Connecting Word)
   3.
      (a)
      (b)
      (c)
      (d)
Illustration/Application?
T.S.(Includes Connecting Word)
   4.   additional points . . . .
Conclusion:Closing prayer

Appendix C: Sermon Unity - Connecting Word Examples

Following are some examples of the relationship between sermon propositions, connecting words and the sermon main points.

The Connecting Word is a plural noun that describes each of the main points of the sermon. The connecting word is often used in transition sentences between major parts of the sermon and serves to help unify the sermon.

Text: Matthew 26:17-30
Proposition: True Fellowship comes easy; requires effort & has risks
Purpose: people will have increased appreciation for fellowship
Connecting Word: elements
Main Points
1. Fellowship is sharing that which we have in common
2. Fellowship requires preparation and focus
3. Fellowship requires sharing of personal information
4. Fellowship makes vulnerable to betrayal and hurt
5. Fellowship makes lifelong and significant memories
6. Fellowship means we rejoice and praise God together

Text: Matthew 26:30-46
Proposition: You can trust God fully; (trust people only so far)
Purpose: people will trust God more, realizing that men will fail them.
Connecting Word: shortcomings (of people)
Main Points
1. Sometimes people allow fleshly desires to control them
2. People are fallible – flesh is weak; limited in ability –
3. People have fears and their fears control them at times –
4. People become weary, tired, fatigued and old –

Text: Matthew 26:47-68
Proposition: By Faith you can stand alone.
Purpose: people will commit to standing on the word of God by Faith
Connecting Word: Choices
Main Points
1. We should restrict our actions to that which is consistent to God's Word
2. We should recognize that all things happen according to God's Word
3. We should anticipate the future blessings associated with fulfillment of God's Word

Text: Matthew 26:69-75
Proposition: You stand by grace alone.
Purpose: realize God's grace causes us to stand before Him
Connecting Word: occasions
Main Points
1. God's grace is not removed from us when we sin.
2. God's grace is not removed from us when we repeatedly sin
3. God's grace is not removed when we are controlled by fear
4. God's grace is not removed from us when we are overwhelmed by our sinfulness or failure.

Text: Matthew 27:1-66
Proposition: Jesus died for All people
Purpose: people will see other people as those for whom Christ died.
Connecting Word: categories
Main Points
1. Jesus died for the Self Righteous - Chief Priests
2. Jesus died for the Unfaithful - Judas
3. Jesus died for those who compromise - Pilate
4. Jesus died for criminals - Barabus
5. Jesus died for those who are abusive - Soldiers
6. Jesus died for those who serve when they are compelled – Simon
7. Jesus died for those who go along with the crowd - bystanders

Appendix D - Sample Sermon Outline

PURPOSE: Those present will commit to bring up their children in the Lord
PROPOSITION: the church must teach parents how raise their children for the Lord
CONNECTING WORD: Essentials   Text: Ephesians 6:4

(Approach sentence to get attention) A.S. Ten years ago I planted small fruit trees at my home and now they have grown to be large trees.

INTRO: But I did not just plant them and go away and wait until they were big. .
I protected, pruned, . . .Children are like trees. . . *(leads into text)*

T.S. Today we consider four things essentials *(connecting word)* the church must teach parents *(proposition)* about raising children the way God wants us to. The first essential *(connecting word)* is that . . .

---

1. We must view raising children as primarily a spiritual responsibility

T.S. It is essential *(connecting word)* that we see raising children as a spiritual task. Prop But not only that, we also need to learn from God how to raise children.

2. We must accept the Bible as the authority for raising children

T.S. the first essential *(connecting word)* is that we see raising children as a spiritual issue. 2nd as a *church and individuals, we must believe that God is the authority for raising children. The third essential *connecting word)* is that . . .

> **3. We must give our children everything they need to know the Lord and grow in Him (three words used)**
>
> T.S. Lastly, it is essential (*connecting word)* that . . .
>
> **4. We must abandon practices that frustrate and provoke our children**

T. S. Children are like trees *(related back to introduction)*.
It is essential *(connecting word)* that we nourish them,
prune them, train them and care for them.

> Conclusion: God expects the church to teach parents how to raise children (*proposition*). God expects parents to put the spiritual well being of the child before everything else in life so that the child may be saved and be able to live a godly life in an ungodly world. Your children do not belong to you. God has only entrusted them to you for a while. It is your job to raise them for Him. May we be diligent to raise our children for God's Glory.

Appendix E - Sermon and Delivery Evaluation

Assign a point value for each of the following.

Sermon Construction & Unity   30 points _____

Identify and Record each of the following (includes comments):

1. Connecting Word:

2. Proposition:

3. Main Sermon Divisions (Main Points)

Sermon was clearly based on text.   20 points _____

Introduction got attention- introduced sermon   10 points_____

Conclusion ended sermon smoothly   10 points _____

Illustrations related to what was being said.   10 points_____

Application - You know God wants you to do   10 points_____

Body language communicated well   10 points_____

Other Specific Comments:

Total points   100 points possible_____

Appendix F: Basic Parts of Speech

The basic parts of speech/language include nouns, pronouns, verbs, adjectives, adverbs, prepositions, conjunctions and interjections.

<u>Nouns</u> name a person, place, or thing (girl, ship, spoon, tree, elephant)

Most nouns have both a singular and plural form, can be preceded by an article and/or one or more adjectives, and can serve as the head of a noun phrase. A noun or noun phrase can function as a subject, direct object, indirect object, complement, appositive, or object of a preposition. In addition, nouns sometimes modify other nouns to form compound nouns.

<u>Pronouns</u> take the place of a noun (I, you, he, she, it, ours, them)

A pronoun can function as a subject, object, or complement in a sentence. Unlike nouns, pronouns rarely allow modification.

<u>Verbs</u> identify action or state of being (sing, dance, believe, be)

There are two main classes of verbs: (1) the large open class of lexical verbs (also known as main verbs or full verbs--that is, verbs that aren't dependent on other verbs); and (2) the small closed class of auxiliary verbs (also called helping verbs). The two subtypes of auxiliaries are the primary auxiliaries (be, have, and do), which can also act as lexical verbs, and the modal auxiliaries (can, could, may, might, must, ought, shall, should, will, and would). Verbs can display differences in tense, mood, aspect, number, person, and voice.

<u>Adjectives</u> modify nouns (cold, red, lazy, crazy, brilliant)

In addition to their basic forms, most descriptive adjectives have two other forms: comparative and superlative. (great, greater, greatest)

<u>Adverbs</u> modify verbs, adjectives, or adverbs (softly, lazily, often)

An adverb that modifies an adjective ("quite sad") or another adverb ("very carelessly") appears immediately in front of the word it modifies. An adverb that modifies a verb is generally more flexible: it may appear before or after the verb it modifies ("softly sang" or "sang softly"), or it may appear at the beginning of the sentence ("Softly she sang to the baby"). The position of the adverb may have an effect on the meaning of the sentence.

Prepositions show relationships (up, over, against, by, for, below)

The combination of a preposition and a noun phrase is called a prepositional phrase. Prepositions convey the following relationships: agency (by); comparison (like, as . . . as); direction (to, toward, through); place (at, by, on); possession (of); purpose (for); source (from, out of); and time (at, before, on).

Conjunctions join words, phrases, and clauses (and, but, or, yet)

A sentence style that employs many coordinate conjunctions is called polysyndeton. A sentence style that omits conjunctions between words, phrases, or clauses is called asyndeton. In contrast to coordinating conjunctions, which connect words, phrases, and clauses of equal rank, subordinating conjunctions connect clauses of unequal rank.

Interjections express emotions – (hey, ah, whoops, ouch)

A short utterance that usually expresses emotion and is capable of standing alone. In writing, an interjection is typically followed by an exclamation point.

A sentence is "a complete unit of thought" that includes as a minimum a noun (called the subject) and a verb (called the preposition). Normally, a sentence expresses a relationship, conveys a command, voices a question, or describes someone or something. It begins with a capital letter and ends with a period, question mark, or exclamation mark.

Glossary of Terms

<u>Application</u> is an explanation or understanding of how to act upon or put into practice knowledge obtain from God's Word.

<u>Approach Sentence</u> is a type of Transition Sentence that is the first thing spoken in a sermon in order to gain the audiences attention and transition into the sermon message.

<u>Connecting Word</u> is a plural noun specifically selected that is descriptive of all the main points in a sermon. The Connecting Word ties the sermon proposition and main points together to make the sermon a single message.

<u>Eisegesis</u> is the practice of reading into a text something that was not intended by the original author.

<u>Exegetical Idea</u> is a concise single sentence summary statement that describes the meaning of a particular text of scripture that was intended by the original author.

<u>Exegetical Purpose</u> is the purpose that the original author had for saying what he said in a particular text.

<u>"Good Sermon - Bad Text"</u> is a phrase used to describe a sermon that does not present error but fails to communicate the truth contained in the text which is the object of the sermon.

<u>"Here and Now"</u> is a phrase that focuses on the modern audiences culture, language, setting, etc, in distinction from that of the original author, audience and setting and the modern.

<u>Hermeneutics</u> is the art, science or methodology utilized in interpreting, especially the Bible.

<u>Homiletics</u> is the art of sermon preparation

<u>Interpretation</u> is the process by which the authors intended meaning is understood. Interpretation also refers to the results of that process.

<u>Exegetical Main Idea</u> is the Exegetical Idea.

<u>Sermon Main Idea</u> is a concise single sentence that communicates the single point of the sermon and has been derived from the Exegetical Idea. The Sermon Main Idea is synonymous with the Sermon Proposition, or Proposition

<u>Sermon Proposition</u> is synonymous with the Sermon Main Idea.

<u>Sermon Purpose</u> is a concise single sentence that expresses the preacher's singular purpose for preaching the sermon that has been derived from the Exegetical Purpose of the Sermon Text.

<u>Sermon Text</u> is that portion of scripture from which the sermon is derived.

<u>"Then and There"</u> is a phrase used to distinguish the original author and audience's setting from that of the modern "Here and Now" preacher and audience.

<u>Transition Sentence</u> is a carefully formed sentence that makes a smooth transition from one portion of a sermon to another. The Transition Sentence will often utilize the Connecting Word to help make the transition and emphasize how the main points relate to one another and the Sermon Main Idea.

ABOUT THE AUTHOR

Jeff Mullins is a tent making pastor serving in rural churches in Northwestern Oregon for the past 25 years. During that time he has been actively involved in training men to carefully interpret the Bible and effectively preach including six month long trips to conduct pastoral training in Russia and Africa.

Jeff has has a great passion for God's Word and a fervor careful interpretation and purposeful practical application.

Jeff is a member of the IFCA International and has served as a missionary pastor with Northwest Independent Church Extension (NICE) and has been serving at Canaan Community Church in Deer Island, Oregon for over two decades.

Jeff is married to Mary Mullins since 1979 and they have seven children together, most of whom are actively involved in Christian service.

Jeff is the author of numerous magazine articles and two other books:

Dating and marriage: Avoiding Hell On Earth

Children: Raising or Ruining?

Jeff operates a portable sawmill business Creation Woods (creationwoods.com) to support his family and to be able to contribute to missions work around the world.